MAJOR DOCUMENTS IN AMERICAN ECONOMIC HISTORY

Volume II

Louis M. Hacker

 AN ANVIL ORIGINAL • PUBLISHED BY VAN NOSTRAND

$1.75

THE AUTHOR

LOUIS M. HACKER is one of nation's foremost authorities on the development of capitalist institutions in the United States. His previous books on the subject include *Triumph of American Capitalism, Shaping of the American Tradition,* and *Alexander Hamilton in the American Tradition.* He is also co-author of *The United States Since 1865* and *The United States in the Twentieth Century.*

Dr. Hacker studied at Columbia University, receiving his A.B. in 1920 and his M.A. in 1923. He also holds the honorary degree LL.D. from the University of Hawaii. After several years of editorial work, he joined the Columbia faculty in 1935 as lecturer in economics. Since 1948 he has been full professor. He was director of the School of General Studies, 1949-1952, and served as dean of that School from 1952 to 1958.

Dr. Hacker has lectured at Cambridge University, the Army War College and the National War College. He also held the Harmsworth chair in American History at Oxford, 1948-1949, and was a Guggenheim fellow.

MAJOR DOCUMENTS
IN AMERICAN ECONOMIC
HISTORY

Vol. II: The Problems of a World Power (The 20th Century)

LOUIS M. HACKER

Professor of Economics
Columbia University

AN ANVIL ORIGINAL
under the general editorship of
LOUIS L. SNYDER

D. VAN NOSTRAND COMPANY, INC.
PRINCETON, NEW JERSEY
TORONTO   LONDON   MELBOURNE

To
Helen
and
Phillip W. Haberman

56687

VAN NOSTRAND REGIONAL OFFICES:
New York, Chicago, San Francisco

D. VAN NOSTRAND COMPANY, LTD., *London*

D. VAN NOSTRAND COMPANY, (Canada), LTD., *Toronto*

D. VAN NOSTRAND AUSTRALIA PTY. LTD., *Melbourne*

Published simultaneously in Canada by
D. VAN NOSTRAND COMPANY (Canada), LTD.

PRINTED IN THE UNITED STATES OF AMERICA

PREFACE

Volume II of this collection treats those very complex concerns of a nation that has reached high maturity in its development, with all those instabilities that beset an industrialized, urbanized, and international economy. Large integrations of capital have appeared; the banking arrangements of an earlier time can no longer serve; labor clamors for legal recognition; and prolonged depression requires the intervention of government to restore social balances and prevent the economy from succumbing to long cyclical swings. At the same time the United States emerges from World War I as a creditor nation—and by the end of the 1950's has more than 64 billion dollars invested abroad, to create another influence that endangers the dollar. Public authority, as in the nineteenth century, continues to preoccupy itself with the problems of Land and Agriculture, Manufactures, Labor and Immigration, Transportation, and Money and Banking; but with a difference. Not only is the scale larger; the involvement of government directly is constant and at many points decisive. With instabilities and despite public intervention, the United States has become a mighty power—and its accomplishments are watched and have repercussions the world over.

Louis M. Hacker

3

TABLE OF CONTENTS

5

— 1 —

ADVANTAGES AND DISADVANTAGES OF LARGE COMBINATIONS, 1900[1]

On June 18, 1898, Congress authorized the establishment of a joint commission of the House and Senate, with nine public members as well, to investigate the impact of industrialization and business combinations on all the aspects of American life. It did so with great competence, publishing 19 volumes in all. This is what the Commission had to say about the new giant corporations just beginning to make their appearance, as they ended the fierce era of competition that had characterized earlier American industrial development.

✓   ✓   ✓

SUMMARY OF ADVANTAGES AND EVILS

I. ADVANTAGES

Those who advocate the formation of large industrial combinations claim that they possess over the system of production on a smaller scale by competing plants the following advantages:

1. *Concentration.*—By closing individual plants less favorably located or less well equipped and concentrating production into the best plants most favorably located a great saving can be effected, both in the amount of capital necessary for the production of a given product and the amount of labor required.

[1] Industrial Commission. *Preliminary Report on Trusts and Industrial Combinations* (March 1, 1900), 56th Congress, 1st Session, House Report 476, Pt. I., pp. 32-35.

Another advantage of the concentration of industry is that the plants which are kept employed can be run at their full capacity instead of at part capacity, and can largely be run continuously instead of intermittently, so far as the combination happens to control the larger part of the entire output—a material source of saving in certain lines of industry. A still further advantage of this concentration comes in the selling of the product, from the fact that customers, being always sure of ready supply whenever it is wanted, more willingly buy from the large producer, and that there is less loss from bad debts. This readiness to buy from trusts, however, is denied, some witnesses holding that dealers prefer to buy from independent producers. . . .

2. *Freights.*—Where the product is bulky, so that the freight forms an essential element of the cost, much can be saved by an organization which has plants established at favorable locations in different sections of the country so that purchasers can be supplied from nearest plants, thus saving the cross freights, which, of course, must be paid where customers are supplied from single competing plants.

3. *Patents and brands.*—Where different establishments, selling separate brands, are brought together into one combination, the use of each brand being made common to all, a great saving is often effected, since the most successful can be more efficiently exploited.

The control also of substantially all patents in one line of industry sometimes enables the combination to secure a monopoly which it could not otherwise secure.

4. *Single management.*—The great completeness and simplicity of the operation of a single great corporation or trust is also a source of saving. Where each of the different establishments which are united had before a president, a complete set of officers, and a separate office force, the combined establishment need have but its one set of chief officers, and subordinates at lesser salaries may take the places of the heads of separate establishments. . . .

The more complete organizations also will distribute the work among the different plants in such a way that to each is given the particular kind of product for which it is specially adapted, and in many cases changes in machinery and changes of workmen from one kind of product to another are avoided, a source often of great saving.

5. *Skilled management.*—The bringing into cooperation of leading men from the separate establishments, each having different elements of skill and experience, makes it possible to apply to the business the aggregate ability of all, a factor in many instances doubtless of great advantage. To some degree there may be a finer specialization of business ability, each man being placed at the head of the department for which he is specially fitted, thus giving, of course, the most skilled management possible to the entire industry, whereas before the combination was effected only a comparatively few of the leading establishments would have managers of equal skill.

But this advantage, some think, is limited. The chief managers at the central office are likely to be large stockholders, and thus to have a strong direct interest in the success of the enterprise. This may hold also of many of the superintendents of departments. But others will be hired managers, and, it is claimed, a hired superintendent will not take the same interest in the establishment or be able to exert the same intelligent control as the owner of a comparatively small establishment. Moreover, minute supervision can not well be exercised in a very large combination.

6. *Export trade.*—The control of large capital also, it is asserted, enables the export trade to be developed to much greater advantage than could be done by smaller establishments with less wealth at their disposal.

II. EVILS

Among the evils of the great combinations those most frequently mentioned are:

1. *Employees discharged.*—When different establishments come together into one, it is often the case that certain classes of employees are needed in much less numbers than by the independent plants. This is specially true in the case of commercial travelers, and, also, perhaps in the case of superintendents and clerks in the offices. While this is generally admitted, it is considered by many to be an inevitable condition of progress and only a temporary hardship which, like that resulting from the introduction of a new machine, will ultimately result in a greater gain.

2. *Methods of competition.*—The large establishments

by cutting prices in certain localities, while maintaining the prices in the main, have a decided advantage over the smaller competitors whose market is limited to the one field in which the prices are cut, and consequently can often succeed in driving their rivals out of the business.

Connected with this method of competition is also the use of unfair methods, such as following up rivals' customers, bribing employees of rivals to furnish information, etc.

The sudden raising and lowering of prices by the combinations, without notice and apparently arbitrarily to embarrass their opponents, is also considered a great evil.

3. *Increased prices.*—When the combinations have sufficient strength, or for any reason get monopolistic control more or less complete, it is thought that they often raise prices above competitive rates, to the great detriment of the public.

4. *Speculation and overcapitalization.*—Another evil often charged against these newer combinations is that the promoter, by virtue of misrepresentations or by the concealment of material facts, is frequently able to secure very large profits for himself at the expense of the people at large who buy the stocks, and that in this way undue speculation is encouraged.

Connected with this evil which comes with the modern method of promotion is that of overcapitalization. Stock is frequently issued to four or five, or even more, times the amount of the cash value of the plants that are brought into the combinations. These stocks then placed upon the market go into the hands of persons ignorant of the real value of the property, who afterwards are likely to lose heavily. Pools are sometimes made to control the stock market, or other of the common ways of disposing of the stock by unfair methods are employed.

At times also the officers and directors of the large combinations seem to have taken advantage of their inside knowledge of the business to speculate on the stock exchange in their own securities to the great detriment of the other shareholders.

5. *Freight discriminations.*—Among the chief evils mentioned are those of freight discriminations in favor of the large companies, which many assert are the chief cause for the growth of the great combinations.

6. *Monopoly; its social effects.*—The fact that an organization possesses a practical monopoly and can in that way direct its operations at the expense of its rivals, thereby preventing competitors from coming into the field, it is thought, takes away from the individual initiative of business men and prevents particularly the younger men from going into business independently. The formerly independent heads of establishments entering the combinations are also, it is said, reduced to the position of hired subordinates. By these means, witnesses claim, the trusts are in reality sapping the courage and power of initiative of perhaps the most active and influential men in the community. This evil is denied by many of the members of the large corporations, who think that within those corporations are found opportunities for the exercise of judgment and enterprise and for rising in life which do not exist outside.

— 2 —

LABOR AND THE FOURTEENTH AMENDMENT, 1905 AND 1940[2]

Beginning with the late 1880's and continuing well into the third decade of the twentieth century, the United States Supreme Court used the due process clause of the Fourteenth Amendment, interpreted substantively, to prevent the States from passing welfare legislation. An outstanding such case was Lochner v. New York (1905), with Justice Holmes dissenting, in which the Court found a New York statute, seeking to regulate the hours of labor in bakeries, unconstitutional because it violated the freedom of contract. By the 1940's, the Court had yielded com-

[2] *198 U. S. 45* (1905) ; *309 U. S. 227* (1940).

pletely; in fact, it was prepared to give a wholly procedural interpretation to the Fourteenth Amendment. This it did in Chambers v. Florida (1940).

✓   ✓   ✓

LOCHNER V. NEW YORK

[Mr. Justice Peckham] . . . . when the State, by its legislature, in the assumed exercise of its police powers, has passed an act which seriously limits the right to labor or the right of contract in regard to their means of livelihood between persons who are *sui juris* (both employer and employee), it becomes of great importance to determine which shall prevail—the right of the individual to labor for such time as he may choose, or the right of the State to prevent the individual from laboring or from entering into contracts to labor, beyond a certain time prescribed by the State.

This court has recognized the existence and upheld the exercise of the police powers of the States in many cases which might fairly be considered as border ones, and it has, in the course of its determination of questions regarding the asserted invalidity of such statutes, on the ground of their violation of the rights secured by the Federal Constitution, been guided by rules of a very liberal nature, the application of which has resulted, in numerous instances, in upholding the validity of state statutes thus assailed. . . .

It must, of course, be conceded that there is a limit to the valid exercise of the police power by the State. . . . In every case that comes before this court, therefore, where legislation of this character is concerned and where the protection of the Federal Constitution is sought, the question necessarily arises: Is this a fair, reasonable and appropriate exercise of the police power of the State, or is it an unreasonable, unnecessary and arbitrary interference with the right of the individual to his personal liberty or to enter into those contracts in relation to labor which may seem to him appropriate or necessary for the support of himself and his family? Of course the liberty of contract relating to labor includes both parties to it. The one has as much right to purchase as the other to sell labor. . . .

The question whether this act is valid as a labor law, pure and simple, may be dismissed in a few words. There is no reasonable ground for interfering with the liberty of person or the right of free contract, by determining the hours of labor, in the occupation of a baker. There is no contention that bakers as a class are not equal in intelligence and capacity to men on other trades or manual occupations, or that they are not able to assert their rights and care for themselves without the protecting arm of the State, interfering with their independence of judgment and of action. They are in no sense wards of the State. . . .

The law must be upheld, if at all, as a law pertaining to the health of the individual engaged in the occupation of a baker. . . .

We think that there can be no fair doubt that the trade of a baker, in and of itself, is not an unhealthy one to that degree which would authorize the legislature to interfere with the right to labor, and with the right of free contract on the part of the individual, either as employer or employee. In looking through statistics regarding all trade and occupations, it may be true that the trade of a baker does not appear to be as healthy as some other trades, and is also vastly more healthy than still others. To the common understanding the trade of a baker has never been regarded as an unhealthy one. . . . It might be safely affirmed that almost all occupations more or less affect the health. . . . But are we all, on that account, at the mercy of the legislative majorities?

Statutes of the nature of that under review, limiting the hours in which grown and intelligent men may labor to earn their living, are mere meddlesome interferences with the rights of the individual, and they are not saved from condemnation by the claim that they are passed in the exercise of the police power and upon the subject of the health of the individual whose rights are interfered with, unless there be some fair ground, reasonable in and of itself, to say that there is material danger to the public health or to the health of the employees, if the hours of labor are not curtailed. If this be not clearly the case the individuals, whose rights are thus made the subject of legislative interference, are under the protection of the Federal Constitution regarding their liberty of contract as well as of person; and the legislature of the State has no power to limit their rights as proposed in this statute. . . .

It is impossible for us to shut our eyes to the fact that many of the laws of this character, while passed under what is claimed to be the police power for the purpose of protecting the public health or welfare, are, in reality, passed from other motives. We are justified in saying so when, from the character of the law and the subject upon which it legislates, it is apparent that the public health or welfare bears but the most remote relation to the law. The purpose of a statute must be determined from the natural and legal effect of the language employed; and whether it is or is not repugnant to the Constitution of the United States must be determined from the natural effect of such statutes when put into operation, and not from their proclaimed purpose. . . .

[Mr. Justice Holmes,, dissenting] . . . . This case is decided upon an economic theory which a large part of the country does not entertain. If it were a question whether I agreed with that theory, I should desire to study it further and long before making up my mind. But I do not conceive that to be my duty, because I strongly believe that my agreement or disagreement has nothing to do with the right of a majority to embody their opinions in law. . . . The Fourteenth Amendment does not enact Mr. Herbert Spencer's Social Statics. . . . A constitution is not intended to embody a particular economic theory, whether of paternalism and the organic relation of the citizen to the state or of *laissez faire*. It is made for people of fundamentally differing views, and the accident of our finding certain opinions natural and familiar, or novel, and even shocking, ought not to conclude our judgment upon the question whether statutes embodying them conflict with the Constitution of the United States.

General propositions do not decide concrete cases. The decision will depend on a judgment or intuition more subtle than any articulate major premise. But I think that the proposition just stated, if it is accepted, will carry us toward the end. Every opinion tends to become a law. I think that the word liberty in the Fourteenth Amendment is perverted when it is held to prevent the natural outcome of a dominant opinion, unless it can be said that a rational and fair man necessarily would admit that the statute proposed would infringe fundamental principles as they have been understood by the traditions of our people and our law. . . .

CHAMBERS V. FLORIDA

[Mr. Justice Black] . . . . The scope and operation of the Fourteenth Amendment have been fruitful sources of controversy in our constitutional history. However, in view of its historical setting and the wrongs which called it into being, the due process provision of the Fourteenth Amendment—just as that in the Fifth—has led few to doubt that it was intended to guarantee procedural standards adequate and appropriate, then and thereafter, to protect, at all times, people charged with or suspected of crime by those holding positions of power and authority. Tyrannical governments had immemorially utilized dictatorial criminal procedures and punishment to make scapegoats of the weak, or of helpless political, religious, or racial minorities and those who differed, who would not conform and who resisted tyranny. The instruments of such governments were in the main, two. Conduct, innocent when engaged in, was subsequently made by fiat criminally punishable without legislation. And a liberty loving people won the principle that criminal punishments could not be inflicted save for that which proper legislative action had already by "the law of the land" forbidden when done. But even more was needed. From the popular hatred and abhorrence of illegal confinement, torture, and extortion of confessions of violations of the "law of the land" evolved the fundamental idea that no man's life, liberty, or property be forfeited as criminal punishment for violation of that law until there had been a charge fairly made and fairly tried in a public tribunal free of prejudice, passion, excitement, and tyrannical power. Thus, as assurance against ancient evils, our country, in order to preserve "the blessings of liberty," wrote into its basic law the requirement, among others, that the forfeiture of the lives, liberties, or property of people accused of crime can only follow if procedural safeguards of due process have been obeyed.

The determination to preserve an accused's right to procedural due process sprang in large part from knowledge of the historical truth that the rights and liberties of people accused of crime could not be safely entrusted to secret inquisitorial processes. The testimony of centuries, in governments of varying kinds over populations of different races and beliefs, stood as proof that physical and mental torture and coercion had brought about the tragically unjust sacrifices of some who were the noblest and most useful of their generations. The rack, the thumbscrew, the wheel, solitary confinement, protracted questioning and cross questioning, and other ingenious forms of entrapment of the helpless or unpopular had left their wake of mutilated bodies and shattered minds along the way to the cross, the guillotine, the stake, and the hangman's noose. And they who have suffered most from secret and dictatorial proceedings have almost always been the poor, the ignorant, the numerically weak, the friendless, and the powerless.

This requirement—of conforming to fundamental standards of procedure in criminal trials—was made operative against the States by the Fourteenth Amendment. . . .

Today, as in ages past, we are not without tragic proof that the exalted power of some governments to punish manufactured crime dictatorially is the handmaid of tyranny. Under our constitutional system, courts stand against any winds that blow as havens of refuge for those who might otherwise suffer because they are helpless, weak, outnumbered, or because they are nonconforming victims of prejudice and public excitement. Due process of law, preserved for all by our Constitution, commands that no such practice as that disclosed by this record shall send any accused to his death. No higher duty, no more solemn responsibility, rests upon this Court, than that of translating into living law and maintaining this constitutional shield deliberately planned and inscribed for the benefit of every human being subject to our Constitution—of whatever race, creed or persuasion.

REPORT ON CONCENTRATION OF MONEY AND CREDIT, BY THE PUJO COMMITTEE, FEBRUARY 28, 1913[3]

It was one of the generally held beliefs of the first decade of the twentieth century that the banking power had become concentrated—that it controlled not only money and credit but also the policies and decisions of the great corporations of the country. A sub-committee of the House Committee on Banking and Currency (controlled by the Democrats after the election of 1910), headed by Congressman Pujo of Louisiana, launched an elaborate inquiry along these lines, issuing its report in 1913 along with four large volumes of testimony. The Committee discovered the concentration of credit it was seeking; and it recommended the abolition of voting trusts and interlocking directorates among national banks, the divorce of security affiliates from the commercial departments of banks, and the banning of financial transactions between banks and their directors. Some of these proposals were embodied in the Clayton Act of 1914, the Transportation Act of 1920, and the Banking Act of 1933. The fact is, however, that one of the casualties of the depression of the 1930's was the loss of the great power the investment houses had exercised over the industrial and railroad companies of America. "Finance Capitalism," so-called, was finished in America.

✓   ✓   ✓

[3] *House Report* 1593 (Money Trust Investigation), 63rd Congress, 3rd Session.

SECTION 1.—TWO KINDS OF CONCENTRATION

It is important at the outset to distinguish between concentration of the *volume of money* in the three central reserve cities of the national banking system—New York, Chicago, and St. Louis—and concentration of *control* of this volume of money and consequently of credit into fewer and fewer hands. They are very different things. An increasing proportion of the banking resources of the country might be concentrating at a given point at the same time that *control* of such resources at that point was spreading out in a wider circle.

Concentration of *control* of money, and consequently of credit, more particularly in the city of New York, is the subject of this inquiry. With concentration of the *volume* of money at certain points, sometimes attributed, so far as it is unnatural, to the provision of the national-banking act permitting banks in the 47 other reserve cities to deposit with those in the three central reserve cities half of their reserves, we are not here directly concerned.

Whether under a different currency system the resources in our banks would be greater or less is comparatively immaterial if they continued to be controlled by a small group. We therefore regard the argument presented to us to show that the growth of concentration of the volume of resources in the banks of New York City has been at a rate slightly less than in the rest of the country, if that be the fact, as not involved in our inquiry. It should be observed in this connection, however, that the concentration of control of credit is by no means confined to New York City, so that the argument is inapplicable also in this respect.

SECTION 2.—FACT OF INCREASING CONCENTRATION ADMITTED

The resources of the banks and trust companies of the city of New York in 1911 were $5,121,245,175, which is 21.73 per cent of the total banking resources of the country as reported to the Comptroller of the Currency. This takes no account of the unknown resources of the great private banking houses whose affiliations to the New York financial institutions we are about to discuss.

That in recent years concentration of control of the banking resources and consequently of credit by the group to which we will refer has grown apace in the city of New York is defended by some witnesses and regretted by others, but acknowledged by all to be a fact.

As appears from statistics compiled by accountants for the committee, in 1911, of the total resources of the banks and trust companies in New York City, the 20 largest held 42.97 per cent; in 1906, the 20 largest held 38.24 per cent of the total; in 1901, 34.97 per cent.

SECTION 3.—PROCESSES OF CONCENTRATION

This increased concentration of control of money and credit has been effected principally as follows:

First, through consolidations of competitive or potentially competitive banks and trust companies, which consolidations in turn have recently been brought under sympathetic management.

Second, through the same powerful interests becoming large stockholders in potentially competitive banks and trust companies. This is the simplest way of acquiring control, but since it requires the largest investment of capital, it is the least used, although the recent investments in that direction for that apparent purpose amount to tens of millions of dollars in present market values.

Third, through the confederation of potentially competitive banks and trust companies by means of the system of interlocking directorates.

Fourth, through the influence which the more powerful banking houses, banks, and trust companies have secured in the management of insurance companies, railroads, producing and trading corporations, and public utility corporations, by means of stockholdings, voting trusts, fiscal agency contracts, or representation upon their boards of directors, or through supplying the money requirements of railway, industrial, and public utilities corporations and thereby being enabled to participate in the determination of their financial and business policies.

Fifth, through partnership or joint account arrangements between a few of the leading banking houses, banks, and trust companies in the purchase of security issues of the great interstate corporations, accompanied by understandings of recent growth—sometimes called "banking ethics"—which have had the effect of effectually destroying competition between such banking houses, banks, and trust companies in the struggle for business or in the purchase and sale of large issues of such securities.

SECTION 4.—AGENTS OF CONCENTRATION

It is a fair deduction from the testimony that the most active agents in forwarding and bringing about the concentration of control of money and credit through one or another of the processes above described have been and are—

J. P. Morgan & Co.
First National Bank of New York.
National City Bank of New York.
Lee, Higginson & Co., of Boston and New York.
Kidder, Peabody & Co., of Boston and New York.
Kuhn, Loeb & Co. . . .

SECTION 5.—J. P. MORGAN & CO.

Organization.—J. P. Morgan & Co. of New York and Drexel & Co. of Philadelphia are one and the same firm, composed of 11 members: J. P. Morgan, E. T. Stotesbury, Charles Steele, J. P. Morgan, jr., Henry P. Davison, Arthur E. Newbold, William P. Hamilton, William H. Porter, Thomas W. Lamont, Horatio G. Lloyd, and Temple Bowdoin. George W. Perkins was a member from 1902 until January 1, 1911. As a firm, it is a partner in the London banking house of J. S. Morgan & Co. and the Paris house of Morgan, Harjes & Co.

General character of business.—It accepts deposits and pays interest thereon and does a general banking business. It is a large lender of money on the New York Stock Exchange. More especially it acts as a so-called issuing house for securities; that is, as purchaser or underwriter or fiscal agent, it takes from the greater corporations their issues of securities and finds a market for them either amongst other banking houses, banks and trust companies, or insurance companies, or the general public.

Resources, deposits, and profits.—Neither the resources and profits of the firm nor its sources of profit have been disclosed. Nor has your committee been able to ascertain its revenues from private purchases or sales of the securities of interstate corporations, nor from such of them as it controls under voting trusts, exclusive fiscal agency agreements, or other arrangements or influences, nor the identity of the banks, trust companies, life insurance companies, or other corporations that have participated in its security issues except where they were for joint account.

On November 1, 1912, it held deposits of $162,491,-819.65, of which $81,968,421.47 was deposited by 78 interstate corporations on the directorates of 32 of which it was represented. The committee is unable to state the character of its affiliations, if any, with the 46 corporations on the directorates of which it is unrepresented by one or more members of the firm, as their identity was not disclosed.

Security issues marketed.—During the years 1902 to 1912, inclusive, the firm directly procured the public marketing of security issues of corporations amounting in round numbers to $1,950,000,000, including only issues of interstate corporations. . . .

Combined power of Morgan & Co., the First National, and National City Banks.—In earlier pages of the report the power of these three great banks was separately set forth. It is now appropriate to consider their combined power as one group.

First, as regards banking resources:

The resources of Morgan & Co. are unknown; its deposits are $163,000,000. The resources of the First National Bank are $150,000,000 and those of its appendage, the First Security Co., at a very low estimate, $35,000,000. The resources of the National City Bank are $274,000,000; those of its appendage, the National City Co., are unknown, though the capital of the latter is alone $10,000,000. Thus, leaving out of account the very considerable part which is unknown, the institutions composing this group have resources of upward of $632,000,000, aside from the vast individual resources of Messrs. Morgan, Baker, and Stillman.

Further, as heretofore shown, the members of this group, through stock holdings, voting trusts, interlocking directorates, and other relations, have become in some cases the absolutely dominant factor, in others the most important single factor, in the control of the following banks and trust companies in the city of New York:

(a)	Bankers Trust Co., resources............	$ 205,000,000
(b)	Guaranty Trust Co., resources...........	232,000,000
(c)	Astor Trust Co., resources..............	27,000,000
(d)	National Bank of Commerce, resources....	190,000,000
(e)	Liberty National Bank, resources.........	29,000,000
(f)	Chase National Bank, resources..........	150,000,000
(g)	Farmers Loan & Trust Co., resources.....	135,000,000

in all, 7, with total resources of.............. 968,000,000
which, added to the known resources of members of the group themselves, makes........ $1,600,000,000
as the aggregate of known banking resources in the city of New York under their control or influence.

If there be added also the resources of the Equitable Life Assurance Society controlled through stock ownership of J. P. Morgan.... 504,000,000

the amount becomes...................... $2,104,000,000

Second, as regards the greater transportation systems.

(a) Adams Express Co.: Members of the group have two representatives in the directorate of this company.

(b) Anthracite-coal carriers: With the exception of the Pennsylvania and the Delaware & Hudson, the Reading, the Central of New Jersey (a majority of whose stock is owned by the Reading), the Lehigh Valley, the Delaware, Lackawanna & Western, the Erie (controlling the New York, Susquehanna & Western), and the New York, Ontario & Western, afford the only transportation outlets from the anthracite coal fields. As before stated, they transport 80 per cent of the output moving from the mines and own or control 88 per cent of the entire deposits. The Reading, as now organized, is the creation of a member of this banking group—Morgan & Co. One or more members of the group are stockholders in that system and have two representatives in its directorate; are stockholders of the Central of New Jersey and have four representatives in its directorate; are stockholders of the Lehigh Valley and have four representatives in its directorate; are stockholders of the Delaware, Lackawanna & Western and have nine representatives in its directorate; are stockholders of the Erie and have four representatives in its directorate; have two representatives in the directorate of the New York, Ontario & Western; and have purchased or marketed practically all security issues made by these railroads in recent years.

(c) Atchison, Topeka & Santa Fe Railway: One or more members of the group are stockholders and have two representatives in the directorate of the company; and since 1907 have purchased or procured the marketing of its security issues to the amount of $107,244,000.

(d) Chesapeake & Ohio Railway: Members of the group have two directors in common with this company, and since 1907, in association with others, have purchased or procured the marketing of its security issues to the amount of $85,000,000.

(e) Chicago Great Western Railway: Members of the group absolutely control this system through a voting trust.

(f) Chicago, Milwaukee & St. Paul Railway: Members of the group have three directors or officers in common with this company, and since 1909, in association with others, have purchased or procured the marketing of its security issues to the amount of $112,000,000.

(g) Chicago & Northwestern Railway: Members of the group have three directors in common with this company, and since 1909, in association with others, have purchased or procured the marketing of its security issues to the amount of $31,250,000.

(h) Chicago, Rock Island & Pacific Railway: Members of the group have four directors in common with this company.

(i) Great Northern Railway: One or more members of the group are stockholders of and have marketed the only issue of bonds made by this company.

(j) International Mercantile Marine Co.: A member of the group organized this company, is a stockholder, dominates it through a voting trust, and markets its securities.

(k) New York Central Lines: One or more members of the group are stockholders and have four representatives in the directorate of the company, and since 1907 have purchased from or marketed for it and its principal subsidiaries security issues to the extent of $343,000,000, one member of the group being the company's sole fiscal agent.

(*l*) New York, New Haven & Hartford Railroad: One or more members of the group are stockholders and have three representatives in the directorate of the company, and since 1907 have purchased from or marketed for it and its principal subsidiaries security issues in excess of $150,000,000, one member of the group being the company's sole fiscal agent.

(*m*) Northern Pacific Railway: One member of the group organized this company and is its fiscal agent, and one or more members are stockholders and have six representatives in its directorate and three in its executive committee.

(*n*) Southern Railway: Through a voting trust, members of the group have absolutely controlled this company since its reorganization in 1894.

(*o*) Southern Pacific Co.: Until its separation from the Union Pacific, lately ordered by the Supreme Court of the United States, members of the group had three directors in common with this company.

(*p*) Union Pacific Railroad: Members of the group have three directors in common with this company.

Third, as regards the greater producing and trading corporations.

(*a*) Amalgamated Copper Co.: One member of the group took part in the organization of the company, still has one leading director in common with it, and markets its securities.

(*b*) American Can Co.: Members of the group have two directors in common with this company.

(*c*) J. I. Case Threshing Machine Co.: The president of one member of the group is a voting trustee of this company and the group also has one representative in its directorate and markets its securities.

(*d*) William Cramp Ship & Engine Building Co.: Members of the group absolutely control this company through a voting trust.

(*e*) General Electric Co.: A member of the group was one of the organizers of the company, is a stockholder, and has always had two representatives in its directorate, and markets its securities.

(*f*) International Harvester Co.: A member of the group organized the company, named its directorate and the chairman of its finance committee, directed its management through a voting trust, is a stockholder, and markets its securities.

(*g*) Lackawanna Steel Co.: Members of the group have four directors in common with the company and, with associates, marketed its last issue of securities.

(*h*) Pullman Co.: The group has two representatives, Mr. Morgan, and Mr. Baker, in the directorate of this company.

(*i*) United States Steel Corporation: A member of the group organized this company, named its directorate, and the chairman of its finance committee (which also has the powers of an executive committee) is its sole fiscal agent and a stockholder, and has always controlled its management.

Fourth, as regards the greater public utility corporations.

(*a*) American Telephone & Telegraph Co.: One or more members of the group are stockholders, have three representatives in its directorate, and since 1906, with other associates, have marketed for it and its subsidiaries security issues in excess of $300,000,000.

(*b*) Chicago Elevated Railways: A member of the group has two officers or directors in common with the company, and in conjunction with others marketed for it in 1911 security issues amounting to $66,000,000.

(*c*) Consolidated Gas Co. of New York: Members of the group control this company through majority representation on its directorate.

(*d*) Hudson & Manhattan Railroad: One or more members of the group marketed and have large interests in the securities of this company, though its debt is now being adjusted by Kuhn, Loeb & Co.

(*e*) Interborough Rapid Transit Co. of New York: A member of the group is the banker of this company, and the group has agreed to market its impending bond issue of $170,000,000.

(*f*) Philadelphia Rapid Transit Co.: Members of the group have two representatives in the directorate of this company.

(*g*) Western Union Telegraph Co.: Members of the group have seven representatives in the directorate of this company.

Summary of directorships held by these members of the group.—Exhibit 134-B shows the combined directorships in the more important enterprises held by Morgan & Co., the First National Bank, the National City Bank and the Bankers and Guaranty Trust Cos., which latter two, as previously shown, are absolutely controlled by Morgan & Co. through voting trusts. It appears there that firm members or directors of these institutions together hold:

One hundred and eighteen directorships in 34 banks and trust companies having total resources of $2,679,000,000 and total deposits of $1,983,000,000.

Thirty directorships in 10 insurance companies having total assets of $2,293,000,000.

One hundred and five directorships in 32 transportation systems having a total capitalization of $11,784,000,000 and a total mileage (excluding express companies and steamship lines) of 150,200.

Sixty-three directorships in 24 producing and trading corporations having a total capitalization of $3,339,000,000.

Twenty-five directorships in 12 public utility corporations having a total capitalization of $2,150,000,000.

In all, 341 directorships in 112 corporations having aggregate resources or capitalization of $22,245,000,000. . . .

WOODROW WILSON ON TARIFF REFORM, APRIL 8, 1913[4]

President Woodrow Wilson appeared personally before the Congress—at that time a novel procedure—to urge the passage of tariff legislation that would part company with the program of high protectionism begun by the Republican party with the Civil War tariffs. The Payne-Aldrich Tariff of 1909 carried duties that averaged 40.1 per cent on an ad valorem basis; the Underwood Tariff of 1913 (following President Wilson's appeal) reduced the general average to 29.6 per cent.

◆   ◆   ◆

Mr. Speaker, Mr. President, gentlemen of the Congress, I am very glad indeed to have this opportunity to address the two Houses directly and to verify for myself the impression that the President of the United States is a person, not a mere department of the Government hailing Congress from some isolated island of jealous power, sending messages, not speaking naturally and with his own voice—that he is a human being trying to cooperate with other human beings in a common service. After this pleasant experience I shall feel quite normal in all our dealings with one another.

I have called the Congress together in extraordinary session because a duty was laid upon the party now in power at the recent elections which it ought to perform promptly, in order that the burden carried by the people under existing law may be lightened as soon as possible, and in order, also, that the business interests of the coun-

[4] *Congressional Record,* 63rd Congress, 1st Session, Vol. 50, Pt. I, p. 130.

try may not be kept too long in suspense as to what the fiscal changes are to be to which they will be required to adjust themselves. It is clear to the whole country that the tariff duties must be altered. They must be changed to meet the radical alteration in the conditions of our economic life which the country has witnessed within the last generation. While the whole face and method of our industrial and commercial life were being changed beyond recognition the tariff schedules have remained what they were before the change began, or have moved in the direction they were given when no large circumstance of our industrial development was what it is to-day. Our task is to square them with the actual facts. The sooner that is done the sooner we shall escape from suffering from the facts and the sooner our men of business will be free to thrive by the law of nature—the nature of free business—instead of by the law of legislation and artificial arrangement.

We have seen tariff legislation wander very far afield in our day—very far indeed from the field in which our prosperity might have had a normal growth and stimulation. No one who looks the facts squarely in the face or knows anything that lies beneath the surface of action can fail to perceive the principles upon which recent tariff legislation has been based. We long ago passed beyond the modest notion of "protecting" the industries of the country and moved boldly forward to the idea that they were entitled to the direct patronage of the Government. For a long time—a time so long that the men now active in public policy hardly remember the conditions that preceded it—we have sought in our tariff schedules to give each group of manufacturers or producers what they themselves thought that they needed in order to maintain a practically exclusive market as against the rest of the world. Consciously or unconsciously, we have built up a set of privileges and exemptions from competition behind which it was easy by any, even the crudest, forms of combination to organize monopoly; until at last nothing is normal, nothing is obliged to stand the tests of efficiency and economy, in our world of big business, but everything thrives by concerted arrangement. Only new principles of action will save us from a final hard crystallization of monopoly and a complete loss of the influences that quicken enterprise and keep independent energy alive.

It is plain what those principles must be. We must abolish everything that bears even the semblance of privilege or of any kind of artificial advantage, and put our business men and producers under the stimulation of a constant necessity to be efficient, economical, and enterprising, masters of competitive supremacy, better workers and merchants than any in the world. Aside from the duties laid upon articles which we do not, and probably can not, produce, therefore, and the duties laid upon luxuries and merely for the sake of the revenues they yield, the object of the tariff duties henceforth laid must be effective competition, the whetting of American wits by contest with the wits of the rest of the world.

It would be unwise to move toward this end headlong, with reckless haste, or with strokes that cut at the very roots of what has grown up amongst us by long process and at our own invitation. It does not alter a thing to upset it and break it and deprive it of a chance to change. It destroys it. We must make changes in our fiscal laws, in our fiscal system, whose object is development, a more free and wholesome development, not revolution or upset or confusion. We must build up trade, especially foreign trade. We need the outlet and the enlarged field of energy more than we ever did before. We must build up industry as well, and must adopt freedom in the place of artificial stimulation only so far as it will build, not pull down. In dealing with the tariff the method by which this may be done will be a matter of judgment exercised item by item. To some not accustomed to the excitements and responsibilities of greater freedom our methods may in some respects and at some points seem heroic, but remedies may be heroic and yet be remedies. It is our business to make sure that they are genuine remedies. Our object is clear. If our motive is above just challenge and only an occasional error of judgment is chargeable against us, we shall be fortunate.

We are called upon to render the country a great service in more matters than one. Our responsibility should be met and our methods should be thorough, as thorough as moderate and well considered, based upon the facts as they are and not worked out as if we were beginners. We are to deal with the facts of our own day, with the facts of no other, and to make laws which square with those facts. It is best, indeed it is necessary, to begin with the tariff. I will urge nothing upon you now at the opening of your session which can obscure that first object or divert our energies from that clearly defined duty. At a later time I may take the liberty of calling your attention to reforms which should press close upon the heels of the tariff changes, if not accompany them, of which the chief is the reform of our banking and currency laws; but just now I refrain. For the present, I put these matters on one side and think only of this one thing—of the changes in our fiscal system which may best serve to open once more the free channels of prosperity to a great people whom we would serve to the utmost and throughout both rank and file. . . .

— 5 —

THE FEDERAL RESERVE ACT OF DECEMBER 23, 1913[5]

The National Banking System had many shortcomings —it could not mobilize reserves and use them effectively; it had no central banking mechanism for expanding and contracting credit—and criticism of it steadily mounted. The Populists of the 1890's, for example, looked upon the banks as devices to restrict credit and they wanted them abolished entirely. In 1908, a National Monetary Commission was created to study the banking system. The Commission issued its report in 1912, in which it proposed the creation of a central bank of issue and rediscount, to be

[5] U. S. Statutes at Large, Vol. 38, 63rd Congress, 2nd Session, Ch. 6, pp. 252-266.

chartered for 50 years and to be called the National Reserve Association. The Association was to be privately controlled; the proposal also failed to come to grips with the inadequacies of the reserve city deposit system.

Congressional Democrats, in 1913, were all opposed to the National Monetary Commission bill, but they could not agree among themselves as to the kind of central bank (and the nature of government participation) to be established. President Wilson intervened, with the support of Secretary of State Bryan, and the bill introduced by Carter Glass in the House was driven through and enacted. The Glass bill differed from the National Monetary Commission bill in these important particulars: the Reserve System was not to be controlled by the member banks; a decentralized system was set up; and a more liberal scheme for currency was provided. All national banking associations were required to become members of the system, and they were to subscribe to the capital stock of the Federal reserve banks "in a sum equal to 6 per cent of the paid-up capital stock and surplus of such bank . . . said payments to be in gold or gold certificates."

An Act to provide for the establishment of Federal reserve banks, to furnish an elastic currency, to afford means of rediscounting commercial paper, to establish a more effective supervision of banking in the United States, and for other purposes. . . .

FEDERAL RESERVE BOARD

SEC. 10. A Federal Reserve Board is hereby created which shall consist of seven members, including the Secretary of the Treasury and the Comptroller of the Currency, who shall be members ex officio, and five members appointed by the President of the United States, by and with the advice and consent of the Senate. In selecting the five appointive members of the Federal Reserve Board, not more than one of whom shall be selected from any one Federal reserve district, the President shall have due regard to a fair representation of the different commercial, industrial and geographical divisions of the country. . . .

The members of said board, the Secretary of the Treasury, the Assistant Secretaries of the Treasury, and the Comptroller of the Currency shall be ineligible during the time they are in office and for two years thereafter to hold any office, position, or employment in any member bank. Of the five members thus appointed by the President at least two shall be persons experienced in banking or finance. One shall be designated by the President to serve for two, one for four, one for six, one for eight, and one for ten years, and thereafter each member so appointed shall serve for a term of ten years unless sooner removed for cause by the President. Of the five persons thus appointed, one shall be designated by the President as governor and one as vice governor of the Federal Reserve Board. The governor of the Federal Reserve Board, subject to its supervision, shall be the active executive officer. . . .

Sec. 11. The Federal Reserve Board shall be authorized and empowered:

(a) To examine at its discretion the accounts, books and affairs of each Federal reserve bank and of each member bank and to require such statements and reports as it may deem necessary. The said board shall publish once each week a statement showing the condition of each Federal reserve bank and a consolidated statement for all Federal reserve banks. . . .

(b) To permit, or, on the affirmative vote of at least five members of the Reserve Board to require Federal reserve banks to rediscount the discounted paper of other Federal reserve banks at rates of interest to be fixed by the Federal Reserve Board.

(c) To suspend for a period not exceeding thirty days, and from time to time to renew such suspension for periods not exceeding fifteen days, any reserve requirement specified in this Act: *Provided,* That it shall establish a graduated tax upon the amounts by which the reserve requirements of this Act may be permitted to fall below the level hereinafter specified: *And provided further,* That when the gold reserve held against Federal reserve notes falls below forty per centum, the Federal Reserve Board shall establish a graduated tax of not more than one per centum per annum upon such deficiency until the reserves fall to thirty-two and one-half per centum, and when said reserve falls below thirty-two and one-half per centum, a tax at the rate increasingly of not less than one and one-half per centum per annum upon each two and one-half per centum or fraction thereof that such reserve falls below thirty-two and one-half per centum. The tax shall be paid by the reserve bank, but the reserve bank shall add an amount equal to said tax to the rates of interest and discount fixed by the Federal Reserve Board.

(d) To supervise and regulate through the bureau under the charge of the Comptroller of the Currency the issue and retirement of Federal reserve notes, and to prescribe rules and regulations under which such notes may be delivered by the Comptroller to the Federal reserve agents applying therefor.

(e) To add to the number of cities classified as reserve and central reserve cities under existing law in which national banking associations are subject to the reserve requirements set forth in section twenty of this Act; or to reclassify existing reserve and central reserve cities or to terminate their designation as such. . . .

POWERS OF FEDERAL RESERVE BANKS

SEC. 13. Any Federal reserve bank may receive from any of its member banks, and from the United States, deposits of current funds in lawful money, national-bank notes, Federal reserve notes, or checks and drafts upon solvent member banks, payable upon presentation; or, solely for exchange purposes, may receive from other Federal reserve banks deposits of current funds in lawful money, national-bank notes, or checks and drafts upon solvent member or other Federal reserve banks, payable upon presentation.

Upon the indorsement of any of its member banks, with a waiver of demand, notice and protest by such bank, any Federal reserve bank may discount notes, drafts, and bills of exchange arising out of actual commercial transactions; that is, notes, drafts, and bills of exchange issued or drawn for agricultural, industrial, or commercial purposes, or the proceeds of which have been used, or are to be used, for such purposes, the Federal Reserve Board to have the right to determine or define the character of the paper thus eligible for discount, within the meaning of this Act.

Nothing in this Act contained shall be construed to prohibit such notes, drafts, and bills of exchange, secured by staple agricultural products, or other goods, wares, or merchandise from being eligible for such discount; but such definition shall not include notes, drafts, or bills covering merely investments or issued or drawn for the purpose of carrying or trading in stocks, bonds, or other investment securities, except bonds and notes of the Government of the United States. Notes, drafts, and bills admitted to discount under the terms of this paragraph must have a maturity at the time of discount of not more than ninety days: *Provided,* That notes, drafts, and bills drawn or issued for agricultural purposes or based on live stock and having a maturity not exceeding six months may be discounted in an amount to be limited to a percentage of the capital of the Federal reserve bank, to be ascertained and fixed by the Federal Reserve Board.

Any Federal reserve bank may discount acceptances which are based on the importation or exportation of goods and which have a maturity at time of discount of not more than three months, and indorsed by at least one member bank. The amount of acceptances so discounted shall at no time exceed one-half the paid-up capital stock and surplus of the bank for which the rediscounts are made. . . .

Any member bank may accept drafts or bills of exchange drawn upon it and growing out of transactions involving the importation or exportation of goods having not more than six months sight to run; but no bank shall accept such bills to an amount equal at any time in the aggregate to more than one-half its paid-up capital stock and surplus. . . .

OPEN-MARKET OPERATIONS

Sec. 14. Any Federal reserve bank may, under rules and regulations prescribed by the Federal Reserve Board, purchase and sell in the open market, at home or abroad, either from or to domestic or foreign banks, firms, corporations, or individuals, cable transfers and bankers' acceptances and bills of exchange of the kinds and maturities by this Act made eligible for rediscount, with or without the indorsement of a member bank.

Every Federal reserve bank shall have power:

(a) To deal in gold coin and bullion at home or abroad, to make loans thereon, exchange Federal reserve notes for gold, gold coin, or gold certificates, and to contract for loans of gold coin or bullion, giving therefor, when necessary, acceptable security, including the hypothecation of United States bonds or other securities which Federal reserve banks are authorized to hold;

(b) To buy and sell, at home or abroad, bonds and notes of the United States, and bills, notes, revenue bonds, and warrants with a maturity from date of purchase of not exceeding six months, issued in anticipation of the collection of taxes or in anticipation of the receipt of assured revenues by any State, county, district, political subdivision, or municipality in the continental United States, including irrigation, drainage and reclamation districts, such purchases to be made in accordance with rules and regulations prescribed by the Federal Reserve Board;

(c) To purchase from member banks and to sell, with or without its indorsement, bills of exchange arising out of commercial transactions, as hereinbefore defined;

(d) To establish from time to time, subject to review and determination of the Federal Reserve Board, rates of discount to be charged by the Federal reserve bank for each class of paper, which shall be fixed with a view of accommodating commerce and business;

(e) To establish accounts with other Federal reserve banks for exchange purposes and, with the consent of the Federal Reserve Board, to open and maintain banking accounts in foreign countries, appoint correspondents, and establish agencies in such countries wheresoever it may deem best for the purpose of purchasing, selling, and collecting bills of exchange, and to buy and sell with or without its indorsement, through such correspondents or agencies, bills of exchange arising out of actual commercial transactions which have not more than ninety days to run and which bear the signature of two or more responsible parties.

GOVERNMENT DEPOSITS

Sec. 15. The moneys held in the general fund of the Treasury, except the five per centum fund for the redemption of outstanding national-bank notes and the funds provided in this Act for the redemption of Federal reserve notes may, upon the direction of the Secretary of the Treasury, be deposited in Federal reserve banks, which banks, when required by the Secretary of the Treasury, shall act as fiscal agents of the United States; and the revenues of the Government or any part thereof may be deposited in such banks, and disbursements may be made by checks drawn against such deposits.

No public funds of the Philippine Islands, or of the postal savings, or any Government funds, shall be deposited in the continental United States in any bank not belonging to the system established by this Act: *Provided, however,* That nothing in this Act shall be construed to deny the right of the Secretary of the Treasury to use member banks as depositories.

NOTE ISSUES

SEC. 16. Federal reserve notes, to be issued at the discretion of the Federal Reserve Board for the purpose of making advances to Federal reserve banks through the Federal reserve agents as hereinafter set forth and for no other purpose, are hereby authorized. The said notes shall be obligations of the United States and shall be receivable by all national and member banks and Federal reserve banks and for all taxes, customs, and other public dues. They shall be redeemed in gold on demand at the Treasury Department of the United States, in the city of Washington, District of Columbia, or in gold or lawful money at any Federal reserve bank.

Any Federal reserve bank may make application to the local Federal reserve agent for such amount of the Federal reserve notes hereinbefore provided for as it may require. Such application shall be accompanied with a tender to the local Federal reserve agent of collateral in amount equal to the sum of the Federal reserve notes thus applied for and issued pursuant to such application. The collateral security thus offered shall be notes and bills, accepted for rediscount under the provisions of section thirteen of this Act, and the Federal reserve agent shall each day notify the Federal Reserve Board of all issues and withdrawals of Federal reserve notes to and by the Federal reserve bank to which he is accredited. The said Federal Reserve

Board may at any time call upon a Federal reserve bank for additional security to protect the Federal reserve notes issued to it.

Every Federal reserve bank shall maintain reserves in gold or lawful money of not less than thirty-five per centum against its deposits and reserves in gold of not less than forty per centum against its Federal reserve notes in actual circulation, and not offset by gold or lawful money deposited with the Federal reserve agent. . . . Notes presented for redemption at the Treasury of the United States shall be paid out of the redemption fund and returned to the Federal reserve banks through which they were originally issued, and thereupon such Federal reserve bank shall, upon demand of the Secretary of the Treasury, reimburse such redemption fund in lawful money or, if such Federal reserve notes have been redeemed by the Treasurer in gold or gold certificates, then such funds shall be reimbursed to the extent deemed necessary by the Secretary of the Treasury in gold or gold certificates . . . Federal reserve notes received by the Treasury, otherwise than for redemption, may be exchanged for gold out of the redemption fund hereinafter provided and returned to the reserve bank through which they were originally issued, or they may be returned to such bank for the credit of the United States. Federal reserve notes unfit for circulation shall be returned by the Federal reserve agents to the Comptroller of the Currency for cancellation and destruction.

The Federal Reserve Board shall require each Federal reserve bank to maintain on deposit in the Treasury of the United States a sum in gold sufficient in the judgment of the Secretary of the Treasury for the redemption of the Federal reserve notes issued to such bank, but in no event less than five per centum; but such deposit of gold shall be counted and included as part of the forty per centum reserve hereinbefore required. . . .

THE FEDERAL TRADE COMMISSION ACT OF SEPTEMBER 26, 1914[6]

The reformers of the New Freedom—committed to the reestablishment of small business in the United States— assumed that unfair business practices could be at once identified and quickly terminated by the establishment of an administrative commission. The model, in this case, was the Interstate Commerce Commission; its general ineffectiveness should have given President Wilson and his advisers pause. The high hopes entertained for the Federal Trade Commission were never realized, and its impact on business practices has been slight. What changes have been accomplished for the better—and they have been many—have been through self-policing devices of trade associations themselves.

An act to create a Federal Trade Commission, to define its powers and duties, and for other purposes.

SEC. 5. That unfair methods of competition in commerce are hereby declared unlawful. . . .

Whenever the commission shall have reason to believe that any such person, partnership, or corporation (except banks and common carriers) has been or is using any unfair method of competition in commerce, . . . it shall issue and serve upon such person, partnership, or corporation a complaint stating its charges in that respect, and containing a notice of a hearing. . . . The person, partnership, or corporation so complained of shall have the right to appear . . . and show cause why an order should not be entered by the commission requiring such person,

[6] *U. S. Statutes at Large,* Vol. 38, 63rd Congress, 2nd Session, Ch. 311, pp. 717-721.

partnership, or corporation to cease and desist from the violation of the law so charged in said complaint. . . . If upon such hearing the commission shall be of the opinion that the method of competition in question is prohibited by this Act, it shall make a report in writing in which it shall state its findings as to the facts, and shall issue and cause to be served on such person, partnership, or corporation an order requiring such person, partnership, or corporation to cease and desist from using such method of competition. . . .

If such person, partnership, or corporation fails or neglects to obey such order of the commission while the same is in effect, the commission may apply to the circuit court of appeals of the United States within any circuit where the method of competition in question is used or where such person, partnership, or corporation resides and carries on business, for the enforcement of its order, and shall file with its application a transcript of the entire record in the proceeding, including all the testimony taken and the report of the commission. Upon such filing of the application and transcript the court shall cause notice thereof to be served upon such person, partnership, or corporation and thereupon shall have jurisdiction of the proceeding and of the question determined therein, and shall have power to make and enter upon the pleadings, testimony, and proceedings set forth in such transcript a decree affirming, modifying and setting aside the order of the commission. The findings of the commission as to the facts, if supported by testimony, shall be conclusive. . . . The judgment and decree of the court shall be final, except that the same shall be subject to review by the Supreme Court upon certiorari as provided in section two hundred and forty of the Judicial Code.

Any party required by such order of the commission to cease and desist from using such method of competition may obtain a review of such order in said circuit court of appeals by filing in the court a written petition praying that the order of the commission be set aside. A copy of such petition shall be forthwith served upon the commission, and thereupon the commission forthwith shall certify and file in the court a transcript of the record as hereinbefore provided. Upon the filing of the transcript the court shall have the same jurisdiction to affirm, set aside, or modify the order of the commission as in the case of an application by the commission for the enforcement of its order, and the findings of the commission as to the facts, if supported by testimony, shall in like manner be conclusive.

The jurisdiction of the circuit court of appeals of the United States to enforce, set aside, or modify orders of the commission shall be exclusive. . . .

Sec. 6. That the commission shall also have power—

(a) To gather and compile information concerning, and to investigate from time to time the organization, business, conduct, practices, and management of any corporation engaged in commerce, excepting banks and common carriers subject to the Act to regulate commerce, and its relation to other corporations and to individuals, associations, and partnerships.

(b) To require, by general or special orders, corporations engaged in commerce, excepting banks, and common carriers subject to the Act to regulate commerce, or any class of them, or any of them, respectively, to file with the commission in such form as the commission may prescribe annual or special, or both annual and special, reports or answers in writing to specific questions, furnishing to the commission such information as it may require as to the organization, business, conduct, practices, management, and relation to other corporations, partnerships, and individuals of the respective corporations filing such reports or answers in writing. Such reports and answers shall be made under oath, or otherwise, as the commission may prescribe, and shall be filed with the commission within such reasonable period as the commission may prescribe, unless additional time be granted in any case by the commission.

(c) Whenever a final decree has been entered against any defendant corporation in any suit brought by the United States to prevent and restrain any violation of the antitrust Acts, to make investigation, upon its own initiative, of the manner in which the decree has been or is being carried out, and upon the application of the Attorney General it shall be its duty to make such investigation. It shall transmit to the Attorney General a report

embodying its findings and recommendations as a result
of any such investigation, and the report shall be made
public in the discretion of the commission.

(d) Upon the direction of the President or either House
of Congress to investigate and report the facts relating to
any alleged violations of the antitrust Acts by any corporation.

(e) Upon the application of the Attorney General to
investigate and make recommendations for the readjustment of the business of any corporation alleged to be vio-
lating the antitrust Acts in order that the corporation may
thereafter maintain its organization, management, and
conduct of business in accordance with law.

(f) To make public from time to time such portions of
the information obtained by it hereunder, except trade
secrets and names of customers, as it shall deem expedient
in the public interest; and to make annual and special reports to the Congress. . . .

— 7 —

THE CLAYTON ANTITRUST ACT OF OCTOBER 15, 1914 [7]

*The Sherman Antitrust Act was amplified by Congress
in 1914 in an effort to cope with the new practices that
American business was developing during the first decade
of the twentieth century. Included in the law were the
famous Sections 6 and 20, which organized labor, in a
burst of uncritical enthusiasm, regarded as its "Charter of
Liberties." More legislation was required—the Norris-La
Guardia Anti-Injunction Act of 1932 and the Wagner La-*

[7] *U. S. Statutes at Large,* Vol. 38, 63rd Congress, 2nd Session,
Ch. 323, pp. 730-738.

*bor Relations Act of 1935—before trade union organiza-
tion and activities were legalized.*

✓   ✓   ✓

Sec. 2. (a) That it shall be unlawful for any person
engaged in commerce, in the course of such commerce,
either directly or indirectly, to discriminate in price between different purchasers of commodities of like grade
and quality, where either or any of the purchases involved
in such discrimination are in commerce, where such commodities are sold for use, consumption, or resale within
the United States or any territory thereof or the District
of Columbia or any insular possession in other places under the jurisdiction of the United States, and where the
effect of such discrimination may be substantially to lessen
competition or tend to create a monopoly in any line of
commerce, or to injure, destroy, or prevent competition
with any person who either grants or knowingly receives
the benefit of such discrimination, or with customers of
either of them: *Provided,* That nothing herein contained
shall prevent differentials which make only due allowance
for differences in the cost of manufacture, sale, or delivery
resulting from the differing methods or quantities in which
such commodities are to such purchasers sold or delivered:
Provided, however, That the Federal Trade Commission
may, after due investigation and hearing to all interested
parties, fix and establish quantity limits, and revise the
same as it finds necessary, as to particular commodities or
classes of commodities, where it finds that available purchasers in greater quantities are so few as to render differentials on account thereof unjustly discriminatory or
promotive of monoply in any line of commerce. . . .

(c) That it shall be unlawful for any person engaged
in commerce, in the course of such commerce, to pay or
grant, or to receive or accept, anything of value as a
commission, brokerage, or other compensation, or any
allowance or discount in lieu thereof, except for services
rendered in connection with the sale or purchase of goods,
wares or merchandise, either to the other party to such
transaction or to any agent, representative, or other intermediary therein where such intermediary is acting in fact
for or in behalf, or is subject to the direct or indirect con-

trol, of any party to such transaction other than the person by whom such compensation is so granted or paid. . . .

SEC. 3. That it shall be unlawful for any person engaged in commerce, to lease or make a sale of goods, . . . for use, consumption or resale within the United States, . . . or fix a price charged therefor, or discount from, or rebate upon, such price, on the condition, . . . that the lessee or purchaser thereof shall not use or deal in the goods, . . . or other commodities of a competitor or competitors of the lessor or seller, where the effect of such lease, sale, or contract for sale or such condition, agreement, or understanding may be to substantially lessen competition or tend to create a monopoly in any line of commerce. . . .

SEC. 6. That the labor of a human being is not a commodity or article of commerce. Nothing contained in the antitrust laws shall be construed to forbid the existence and operation of labor, agricultural, or horticultural organizations, instituted for the purposes of mutual help, and not having capital stock or conducted for profit, or to forbid or restrain individual members of such organizations from lawfully carrying out the legitimate objects thereof; nor shall such organizations, or the members thereof, be held or construed to be illegal combinations or conspiracies in restraint of trade, under the antitrust laws.

SEC. 7. That no corporation engaged in commerce shall acquire, directly or indirectly, the whole or any part of the stock or other share capital of another corporation engaged also in commerce, where the effect of such acquisition may be to substantially lessen competition between the corporation whose stock is so acquired and the corporation making the acquisition, or to restrain such commerce in any section or community, or tend to create a monopoly of any line of commerce.

No corporation shall acquire, directly or indirectly, the whole or any part of the stock or other share capital of two or more corporations engaged in commerce where the effect of such acquisition, or the use of such stock by the voting or granting of proxies or otherwise, may be to substantially lessen competition between such corporations, or any of them, whose stock or other share capital is so acquired, or to restrain such commerce in any section or community, or tend to create a monopoly of any line of commerce. . . .

SEC. 8. That from and after two years from the date of the approval of this Act no person shall at the same time be a director or other officer or employee of more than one bank, banking association or trust company, organized or operating under the laws of the United States, either of which has deposits, capital, surplus, and undivided profits aggregating more than $5,000,000; and no private banker or person who is a director in any bank or trust company, organized and operating under the laws of a State, having deposits, capital, surplus, and undivided profits aggregating more than $5,000,000, shall be eligible to be a director in any bank or banking association organized or operating under the laws of the United States. . . .

That from and after two years from the date of the approval of this Act no person at the same time shall be a director in any two or more corporations, any one of which has capital, surplus, and undivided profits aggregating more than $1,000,000, engaged in whole or in part in commerce, other than banks, banking associations, trust companies and common carriers subject to the Act to regulate commerce, approved February fourth, eighteen hundred and eighty-seven, if such corporations are or shall have been theretofore, by virtue of their business and location of operation, competitors, so that the elimination of competition by agreement between them would constitute a violation of any of the provisions of any of the anti-trust laws. . . .

SEC. 10. That after two years from the approval of this Act no common carrier engaged in commerce shall have any dealings in securities, supplies or other articles of commerce, or shall make or have any contracts for construction or maintenance of any kind, to the amount of more than $50,000, in the aggregate, in any one year, with another corporation, firm, partnership or association when the said common carrier shall have upon its board of directors or as its president, manager or as its purchasing or selling officer, or agent in the particular transaction, any person who is at the same time a director, manager, or purchasing or selling officer of, or who has any substantial interest in, such other corporation, firm, partnership or association, unless and except such purchases shall be made from, or such dealings shall be with, the bidder whose bid is the most favorable to such common carrier, to be ascertained by competitive bidding under regulations to be prescribed by rule or otherwise by the Interstate Commerce Commission. No bid shall be received unless the name and address of the bidder or the names and addresses of the officers, directors and general managers thereof, if the bidder be a corporation, or of the members, if it be a partnership or firm, be given with the bid. . . .

SEC. 20. That no restraining order or injunction shall be granted by any court of the United States, or a judge or the judges thereof, in any case between an employer and employees, or between employers and employees, or between employees, or between persons employed and persons seeking employment, involving, or growing out of, a dispute concerning terms or conditions of employment, unless necessary to prevent irreparable injury to property, or to a property right, of the party making the application, for which injury there is no adequate remedy at law, and such property or property right must be described with particularity in the application, which must be in writing and sworn to by the applicant or by his agent or attorney.

And no such restraining order or injunction shall prohibit any person or persons, whether singly or in concert, from terminating any relation of employment, or from ceasing to perform any work or labor, or from recommending, advising, or persuading others by peaceful means so to do; or from attending at any place where any such person or persons may lawfully be, for the purpose of peacefully obtaining or communicating information, or from peacefully persuading any person to work or to abstain from working; or from ceasing to patronize or to employ any party to such dispute, or from recommending, advising, or persuading others by peaceful and lawful means so to do; or from paying or giving to, or withholding from, any person engaged in such dispute, any strike benefits or other moneys or things of value; or from peaceably assembling in a lawful manner, and for lawful purposes; or from doing any act or thing which might lawfully be done in the absence of such dispute by any party thereto; nor shall any of the acts specified in this paragraph be considered or held to be violations of any law of the United States. . . .

— 8 —

REPORT OF THE COMPTROLLER OF THE CURRENCY, DECEMBER 6, 1915 [8]

The Comptroller of the Currency, in his 1915 Report, presented a lucid analysis of the character and shortcomings of the National Banking System and told how the Federal Reserve System met successfully its first test under fire—that of the financial crisis of 1914.

✸   ✸   ✸

THE NATIONAL BANKING SYSTEM

Our National Banking System, established during the Civil War by authority of an act of Congress approved February 25, 1863, was a success and achieved the purposes for which it was primarily created. It furnished the market so much needed at that time for Government bonds which had to be sold to provide funds for the prosecution of the Civil War. It established a uniform currency, which circulated at its face value in every part of the country,

[8] *Annual Report of the Comptroller of the Currency,* to the First Session of the 64th Congress of the United States, December 6, 1915, Vol. 1.

and abolished the so-called "wildcat" currency issued by the State banks in the different States and which sold at nearly as many rates of discount as there were places in which it was circulated.

Every bank of deposit, whether it pays interest on its deposits or whether it does not, must keep on hand, either in its vaults or in some place where it may be readily available, a certain proportion of its deposits to meet the checks which may be drawn upon it by its depositors.

Prior to the inauguration of the Federal Reserve System banks in the three "central reserve" cities of New York, Chicago, and St. Louis were required to keep in their vaults 25 per cent of their deposits in cash. There were also 51 cities known as "reserve" cities, and the national banks in these cities were required to keep a reserve of 25 per cent of their deposits, of which one-half, or 12½ per cent, was carried in their vaults and the other 12½ per cent with their correspondent national banks in any one of the three central reserve cities. All of the other national banks throughout the United States, commonly designated as "country banks," although some of the cities in which these "country banks" were located were larger than some of the "reserve" cities, were required to maintain a reserve equal to 15 per cent of their deposits, of which two-fifths, or 6 per cent, had to be carried in their vaults and the remaining 9 per cent could be carried either in their vaults or could be held for their credit in national banks in either the reserve or central reserve cities.

With the vast development and growth of our agriculture, industry, and commerce the old national banking system became inadequate to meet the needs of business. The demand for money was, in the nature of things, greater at one season of the year than at another, and each recurring autumn, when the crops were to be moved, there was nearly always the same uneasiness—active demand for and insufficiency of money.

When unexpected crises arose, resulting in extraordinary calls for money, the unresponsiveness of our currency became more emphasized. Our bank-note currency, secured by the deposit with the national banks of Government bonds, was inelastic and could not be increased as necessity arose for more money to meet enlarged demands of business.

BANKS COULD NOT ALWAYS RELY ON AVAILABILITY OF THEIR BALANCES WITH RESERVE AGENTS

Experience had shown that the system of accumulating and impounding reserves for the national banks of the reserve cities, as well as those of the country banks, in the three "central reserve" cities of New York, Chicago, and St. Louis worked badly. The funds of the banks throughout the country were stored up and concentrated in these three cities. The banks in these cities, especially in New York, had become accustomed to lending largely in Wall Street on demand, on bond and stock collateral, the reserve balances which these banks held for other banks, and upon which they usually paid the depositing banks 2 per cent per annum interest. Periodically, or in the crop-moving season, when the country banks had to withdraw their deposits from the centers, the national banks in the large cities would call in these loans on bonds and stocks, money rates would advance, and stocks decline. This process went on from year to year.

When there was sudden strain and need, as in 1893 and 1907, the banks throughout the country having or anticipating a demand from their customers for money would seek to draw in their balances from New York and the other large cities. The New York banks, however, at these times unable to meet the demands upon them, would suspend currency shipments and resort to the usual remedy of issuing clearing-house certificates for protection until normal conditions should be resumed, and the banks in other large cities thereupon generally would be forced to follow the lead set by the New York banks, would hold onto the money of their correspondents, and issue clearing-house certificates, while currency was being bought and sold at a premium of 2 to 5 per cent.

AIMS OF FEDERAL RESERVE SYSTEM

The Federal Reserve System has been designed to correct these and other evil and dangerous conditions and to furnish the banks and to the people of the country new and additional banking and financial facilities by providing:

First. A currency or circulating medium which will not only pass without question at its face value in every part of the country, but which will expand when necessary to meet legitimate demands of increasing business, and which will also contract at the proper time when no longer required and when its continuance in circulation would threaten or promote inflation.

Second. An improved system for the management and handling of the bank reserves, whereby these reserves become readily and easily available to meet demands for increased money and credit and where the proper utilization of that portion of the bank reserves not held in the vaults of the respective individual banks may be made available as a means of relief and to prevent the financial crises or market panics from which the country has suffered so often when the country banks have tried to bring home their reserves to meet the wants of their customers.

Third. A clearing or collection system by which the checks on national banks and other banks which are members of the Federal Reserve System, drawn on solvent banks by solvent drawers, may be cashed or collected at par in every part of the country, without the burden and expense of the exchange and collection charges which have been a material expense and a serious drawback to business operations.

Fourth. The Federal reserve banks furnish through their capital, their large deposits, and their note-issuing power the facilities by which all members of the system, in any emergency, may rediscount their eligible paper and obtain funds to meet any sudden or unexpected demands. These reserve banks also provide their member banks in ordinary times with money and credit to enable them to meet the legitimate demands of customers for increased accommodations when the member banks themselves have not the needed funds.

Fifth. The Federal Reserve System, by providing a source from which all well managed banks at all times may secure funds to meet any emergency, makes unnecessary the carrying by member banks of the reserves formerly required for national banks. By the reduction in reserve requirements provided by the act the loanable funds of the national banks upon the inauguration of the Federal Reserve System were increased immediately, through the release of reserves, by an amount figured at considerably more than $400,000,000.

The other direct advantages provided by the Federal reserve act are (a) the opportunity given to national banks under certain conditions to lend money on improved, unincumbered farm property; (b) the power conferred on national banks to establish branches in foreign countries; (c) the establishment and authorization of bank acceptances; (d) the provisions for open-market operations by Federal reserve banks; and, finally (e) the adoption of the new method for the compensation of bank examiners, which insures a more thorough and systematic examination of national banks than was possible under the antiquated fee system.

FINANCIAL CRISIS OF 1914

The Federal Reserve Board was organized August 12, 1914, ten days after the outbreak of the European war, but the Federal reserve banks were not opened for business until November 16, 1914. The commerce, industry, and business of the entire world were disturbed as never before. "Moratoria" had been declared in nearly all foreign countries. Outside sources of relief were shut off and the banking situation was greatly demoralized. As a result, however, of the instant and energetic action of the Secretary of the Treasury, August 2, 1914, authorizing and directing the issue of several hundred million dollars of "emergency currency" under the provisions of the emergency currency law of May 30, 1908, as amended by the Federal reserve act, the banks in all parts of this country—north, east, south, and west—were supplied promptly with all the currency they needed, which enabled them to maintain currency payments throughout the entire country, a record they were unable to make in 1893 and in 1907, and in previous crises infinitely less far-reaching than that which confronted us a year ago.

EFFECTS OF THE NEW BANKING SYSTEM

The New York and other stock exchanges had been closed since July 30, 1914. The general business of the country was in an abnormal condition, for which there was no precedent by which thought and action could be guided. Some bankers and financiers had misgivings as to whether the new financial system ought to be launched under such critical and trying circumstances. Further delay in putting it into effect was being strongly urged. The Secretary of the Treasury, however, having taken all factors into consideration, determined that the sooner the Federal Reserve System could be placed in operation the better it would be for the country; and in accordance with the authority vested in him he announced on the 25th day of October, 1914, that the 12 Federal reserve banks would open for business on November 16, 1914.

It was, therefore, under these stirring and world-shaking conditions that the system had its birth. Its progress from the very start has been steady and enormously beneficial to the banking and business interests of the country.

REVIVAL OF CONFIDENCE AND BUSINESS

From November 16, 1914, to the present time confidence in the strength and soundness of business and financial conditions has grown almost uninterruptedly. All the $318,484,485 of emergency currency which was outstanding on November 16, 1914, when the new system started, had been retired by July 1, 1915, with the exception of $200,000 issued to a failed bank; and this small balance has been paid in full.

The beneficent influences of the Federal reserve act have been exerted in every city, town, and village from one end of the country to the other; and these effects have been realized by business men of all classes, who have been enabled to secure the money needed for their legitimate requirements at rates of interest more favorable than ever known in our history.

Many opponents of the Federal Reserve System, endeavoring to defeat or delay the passage of the act, freely predicted that, if the law should be passed, a commercial

panic would ensue; that the withdrawal of the enormous
bank reserves from New York, Chicago, and St. Louis
would produce convulsions from which the whole country
would suffer. Experience, however, has contradicted these
prophecies squarely. The business and commerce of the
United States have not contracted. They have expanded
to dimensions never before reached.

— 9 —

THE IMMIGRATION ACT OF MAY 26, 1924[9]

*Two different groups, as far back as the 1880's, began
to agitate for limitations to be imposed on free immigration: those who deplored the heterogeneous character of
the new aliens coming from eastern and southern Europe;
and the organized workers who argued that the new immigrants beat down wages and acted as strike breakers. In
1921 Congress finally yielded and passed an immigration
act setting up a quota system which, however, was at-
tacked because it did not favor enough newcomers from
northern and western Europe. The law of 1924 both reduced the quotas and set 1890 (changing this from 1910)
as the basic date on which the formula of "national origins" was set. This naturally discriminated against those
who sought to enter the country from Italy, Greece, Po-
land, Russia, and the like.*

✓   ✓   ✓

It will undoubtedly be considered that the most important event in the immigration history of the fiscal year was

[9] *Annual Report of the Commissioner-General of Immigration*
(1924), pp. 24-30.

the passage of the act of May 26, officially known as the "Immigration act of 1924." This legislation which supplants the so-called quota limit act of May 19, 1921, the latter having expired by limitation at the close of the fiscal year just ended, makes several very important changes not only in our immigration policy but also in the administrative machinery of the Immigration Service. Some of the more important changes in these respects will be briefly referred to.

It will be remembered that the quota limit act of May, 1921, provided that the number of aliens of any nationality admissible to the United States in any fiscal year should be limited to 3 per cent of the number of persons of such nationality who were resident in the United States according to the census of 1910, it being also provided that not more than 20 per cent of any annual quota could be admitted in any one month. Under the act of 1924 the number of each nationality who may be admitted annually is limited to 2 per cent of the population of such nationality resident in the United States according to the census of 1890, and not more than 10 per cent of any annual quota may be admitted in any month except in cases where such quota is less than 300 for the entire year.

Under the act of May, 1921, the quota area was limited to Europe, the Near East, Africa, and Australasia. The countries of North and South America, with adjacent islands, and countries immigration from which was otherwise regulated, such as China, Japan, and countries within the Asiatic barred zone, were not within the scope of the quota law. Under the new act, however, immigration from the entire world, with the exception of the Dominion of Canada, Newfoundland, the Republic of Mexico, the Republic of Cuba, the Republic of Haiti, the Dominican Republic, the Canal Zone, and independent countries of Central and South America, is subject to quota limitations. . . .

The quotas from various countries or regions of birth allotted under the act of May, 1921, the old quota law, and the act of 1924 are shown in the following compilation:

The act of 1924 defines the term "immigrant" as "any alien departing from any place outside the United States

Country or region of birth	Act of 1921	Act of 1924	Country or region of birth	Act of 1921	Act of 1924
Albania......	288	100	Lithuania ...	2,629	344
Armenia			Luxemburg..	92	100
(Russian) ..	230	124	Netherlands .	3,607	1,648
Austria.......	7,342	785	Norway.....	12,202	6,453
Belgium......	1,563	512	Poland......	30,977	5,982
Bulgaria......	302	100	Portugal....	2,465	503
Czechoslovakia	14,357	3,073	Rumania....	7,419	603
Danzig.......	301	228	Russia......	24,405	2,248
Denmark.....	5,619	2,789	Spain.......	912	131
Estonia......	1,348	124	Sweden.....	20,042	9,561
Finland......	3,921	471	Switzerland..	3,752	2,081
France.......	5,729	3,954	Yugoslavia ..	6,426	671
Germany.....	67,607	51,227	Palestine....	57	100
Great Britain,			Syria.......	882	100
Ireland.....	77,342	34,007	Turkey......	2,654	100
Greece.......	3,063	100	Australia....	279	121
Hungary.....	5,747	473	New Zealand		
Iceland.......	75	100	and Pacific		
Irish Free			Islands....	80	100
State*......	.....	28,567	All others ...	492	3,100
Italy.........	42,057	3,845			
Latvia.......	1,540	142	Total...	357,803	164,667

* Included in Great Britain, Ireland, under act of 1921.

destined for the United States, except (1) a Government official, his family, attendants, servants, and employees, (2) an alien visiting the United States temporarily as a tourist or temporarily for business or pleasure, (3) an alien in continuous transit through the United States, (4) an alien lawfully admitted to the United States who later goes in transit from one part of the United States to another through foreign contiguous territory, (5) a bona fide alien seaman serving as such on a vessel arriving at a port of the United States and seeking to enter temporarily the United States solely in the pursuit of his calling as a seaman, and (6) an alien entitled to enter the United States solely to carry on trade under and in pursuance of the provisions of a present existing treaty of commerce and navigation."

Immigrants are, in effect, divided into two classes, quota immigrants and nonquota immigrants, meaning in the first instance aliens who are chargeable against the quotas of their respective countries and in the second immigrants who may enter the United States without reference to quota limitations, the latter including (a) an immigrant who is the unmarried child under 18 years of age, or the wife, of a citizen of the United States who resides therein at the time of the filing of a petition under section 9; (b) an immigrant previously lawfully admitted to the United States, who is returning from a temporary visit abroad; (c) an immigrant who was born in the Dominion of Canada, Newfoundland, the Republic of Mexico, the Republic of Cuba, the Republic of Haiti, the Dominican Republic, the Canal Zone, or an independent country of Central or South America, and his wife, and his unmarried children under 18 years of age, if accompanying or following to join him; (d) an immigrant who continuously for at least two years immediately preceding the time of his application for admission to the United States has been, and who seeks to enter the United States solely for the purpose of carrying on the vocation of minister of any religious denomination, or professor of a college, academy, seminary, or university, and his wife, and his unmarried children under 18 years of age, if accompanying or following to join him; or (e) an immigrant who is a bona fide student at least 15 years of age and who seeks to enter the United States solely for the purpose of study at an accredited school, college, academy, seminary, or university, particularly designated by him and approved by the Secretary of Labor which shall have agreed to report to the Secretary of Labor the termination of attendance of each immigrant student, and if any such institution of learning fails to make such reports promptly the approval shall be withdrawn. All other aliens, except the nonimmigrant classes listed above, are quota immigrants.

All quota and nonquota immigrants must be in possession of an immigration visa issued by a United States consul before they can be admitted to the United States, and the annual and monthly limitation under the various quotas is controlled through limiting the number of quota immigration visas issued in any month or year. In other words, the quotas are counted or controlled in American consulates, usually in the country where the applicant resides, rather than on arrival at a United States port, as was the case under the former quota limit act, thus obviating the unhappy experiences of the past three years, when thousands of aliens were brought to the United States in excess of quotas only to be returned to the country of origin.

Preference in the issuance of quota visas is given to a quota immigrant who is the unmarried child under 21 years of age, the father, the mother, the husband, or the wife, of a citizen of the United States who is 21 years of age or over, and to a quota immigrant who is skilled in agriculture, and his wife, and his dependent children under the age of 16 years, if accompanying or following to join him. A preference in the case of persons skilled in agriculture is not applicable to immigrants of any nationality the annual quota for which is less than 300, and in no case shall the combined preferences exceed 50 per cent of the annual quota of any nationality.

The law provides that on and after July 1, 1927, quotas shall be calculated as provided in section 11 of the act under discussion, which provides in part as follows:

SEC. 11. (a) The annual quota of any nationality shall be 2 per centum of the number of foreign-born individuals of such nationality resident in continental United States as determined by the United States census of 1890, but the minimum quota of any nationality shall be 100.

(b) The annual quota of any nationality for the fiscal year beginning July 1, 1927, and for each fiscal year thereafter, shall be a number which bears the same ratio to 150,000 as the number of inhabitants in continental United States in 1920 having that national origin (ascertained as hereinafter provided in this section) bears to the number of inhabitants in continental United States in 1920, but the minimum quota of any nationality shall be 100.

(c) For the purpose of subdivision (b) national origin shall be ascertained by determining as nearly as may be, in respect of each geographical area which under section 12 is to be treated as a separate country (except the geographical areas specified in subdivision (c) of section 4) the number of inhabitants in continental United States in 1920 whose origin by birth or ancestry is attributable to such geographical area. Such determination shall not be made by tracing the ancestors or descendants of particular individuals, but shall be based upon statistics of immigration and emigration, together with rates of increase of population as shown by successive decennial United States censuses, and such other data as may be found to be reliable. . . .

Another important provision of the act of 1924 is found in section 13, which provides that with certain exceptions "no alien ineligible to citizenship shall be admitted to the United States." The import of this provision will be readily understood when it is considered that the naturalization laws state that the provisions thereof "shall apply to aliens being free white persons and to aliens of African nationality and to persons of African descent." This, in effect, means that persons other than members of the Caucasian, or white, race and of the African, or black, race are not eligible to citizenship through naturalization and, therefore, with certain exceptions, not eligible for admission to the United States as immigrants. Included in the category of persons ineligible to citizenship are the Chinese, Japanese, East Indians, and other peoples indigenous to Asiatic countries and adjacent islands. . . .

— 10 —

RECENT ECONOMIC CHANGES IN THE UNITED STATES, 1929[10]

By the end of the 1920's a golden age of high employment and high national income had been reached: or so it

[10] *Recent Economic Changes in the U. S.* Report of the Committee on Recent Economic Changes of the President's Conference on Unemployment (New York, 1929), Vol. 2, Introduction.

*seemed to the large company of scholars gathered together
to survey the scene under the direction of Professor Edwin
F. Gay of Harvard University. Professor Gay wrote the
general remarks that follow.*

✓   ✓   ✓

. . . During the last six or seven years, books, reports and
articles, in many languages, describing, explaining or criti-
cizing the economic and social situation in the United
States, have appeared in unparalleled quantity. This has
been heralded as the new Discovery of America.

Foreign Opinions.—Despite such divergence of opinion
among these contemporaneous observers as to causes and
conditions, there is marked unanimity as to the fact which
is chiefly responsible for this extraordinary interest. They
agree that of late there has been an "immense advance in
America." Our visitors are "impressed, everywhere and
every day, by the evidences of an ebullient prosperity and
a confidence in the future." . . .

The consensus of foreign opinion concerning the present
great American prosperity is evident to any student of this
recent literature. But, though it might be interesting, it
would certainly be a difficult and a time-consuming task
to trace all the divergences of point of view and the differing degrees of emphasis as to the causes of that prosperity. . . .

America has become the arsenal when weapons are
drawn for both sides of embittered argument. (On the protective tariff, for example, on high wages, on agriculture,
and on standardization.) . . .

It is needless to enlarge on the numerous clashes in the
testimony of the foreign observers. It is more to the
point to indicate that, despite their varying origins and
predilections, there is a considerable degree of concurrence,
although with differing emphasis, regarding certain main
factors in the recent economic and social experience of this
country. These factors may here be briefly summarized.

1. The natural resources of the United States are un-
rivaled, especially those which are fundamental to modern
large-scale industrialism. . . .

2. In this vast expanse of territory, historically so recently opened to European migration and settlement, labor

is relatively scarce and wages are relatively high . . .
there is in the United States a markedly higher standard of
living, and this profoundly influences the American outlook.

3. In consequence of the juxtaposition of rich resources
and an inadequate labor supply, there has resulted a
progressive development of labor-supplementing machine
equipment, in agriculture, transportation and industry, and
also a remarkable utilization of power. . . .

4. Many observers hold that of even greater importance
than the technical progress is the great domestic market. . . . The resulting "mass consumption" makes mass
production possible and profitable. . . .

5. The problem of correlating abundant resources, ex-
pensive labor, and unsurpassed machine equipment, to
serve the greatest of markets, has put a high premium on
management and organizing capacity. . . .

6. In order to obtain the effective utilization of the
worker's effort and to lower costs, American management
has begun more systematically to improve industrial relations. . . .

7. A related factor in American economic efficiency is
the openmindedness of American management. . . .

8. Emphasis is unanimously laid upon the dominant national trait of optimistic energy, as an underlying element
in these various phenomena of American economic activity.
The individual in America is mobile. . . . He sometimes
appears docile, but it is because he is tolerant of social
inconveniences which his experience tells him are only
incidental and temporary. . . .

. . . But it will serve our present purpose to point out
that most of the eight significant features of the existing
economic conditions in the United States upon which we
have found our foreign visitors in substantial agreement
are also characteristic of former major periods of prosperity in our history. The fundamental conditions of our
existence on this continent have thus far remained substantially unchanged, and the responses have therefore
been similar, not so much in external form as in their
essential character. Even the successive maladjustments of
economic growth show, behind their external dissimilari-
ties, an underlying likeness. With superabundant natural

resources, for example, we have always been open to the charge of wastefulness, and this is easily explicable, but with insufficient man power it seems, at first thought, curious that we are now and have ever been wasteful of human life. . . . But there was a sign of change in the fundamental conditions of our natural life when there emerged the conservation movement for the natural resources, and the slogan "safety first" for human life. Another serious maladjustment has been constantly observable in the extreme to which we have carried the swings of prosperity and business depression, the fierce bursts of speculative activity and the sharp reactions. Again, our environment and its needs may help to explain this feverish pulse-beat; yet here also another slogan, "stability," may be symptomatic of coming fundamental change. It is, furthermore, highly characteristic of all our periods of expansion that the rapidity and vigor of growth of some elements is so great as seriously to unbalance the whole organism. . . . With each successive advance, for instance, there has remained a farm problem and agrarian discontent somewhere in the rear. These rough dislocations in the past have made us exceptionally prone to scrap machinery and men. But quick adaptation and rapid mutation, perhaps biologically useful, our industrial society is now commencing to regard with social concern.

The shifting of psychological attitude, here indicated, seems to suggest that something distinctly different from our former experience is taking place. The chief characteristics of the present economic phase, agreed upon by our numerous visitors from abroad, are, it is true, evolved logically from what has preceded. . . . But there seem now to be differences of degree which approach differences in kind. In this sense we may say that the unprecedented utilization of power and its wide dispersion by automobile and tractor, in which this country leads the way, is a new addition of enormous potentiality to our resources. With the general increase of wealth, the growth in the number of millionaires has been accompanied by a remarkable rise in the real wages of industrial workers, and a wide diffusion of investments. The profession of management is clearly emerging, and there is visible an increasing professional spirit in business, which springs from and entails recognized social responsibilities. The "self-policing" of business, with its codes of ethics, has been assisted by the recent development of trade-associations and the increasing influence of research and professional education. The strength and stability of our financial structure, both governmental and commercial, is of modern growth. The great corporate development of business enterprise . . . has gone on to new heights. It may be creating, as some think, a new type of social organization, but in any case the open-mindedness of the public, and of the state which is its instrument, toward this growing power of business corporations appears to be novel in American history.

Here are the beginnings of new answers to the old problem. But more than this. Some of the basic elements of the problem are evidently in process of change. The resources of the country, still enormous, are no longer regarded as limitless; the labor of the world is no longer invited freely to exploit them. The capital flow has turned outward; private and public interests and responsibilities have a new world-wide scope. These changes must have far-reaching consequences and entail further and more perplexing adjustments. . . .

— 11 —

THE NORRIS-LA GUARDIA ANTI-INJUNCTION ACT OF MARCH 23, 1932 [11]

The continued use by the Courts of the injunctive right to limit severely the conduct of trade unions in industrial

[11] *U. S. Statutes at Large,* Vol. 47, 72nd Congress, 1st Session, Ch. 90, pp. 70-73.

disputes had led to repeated efforts to untie the hands of organized labor. The provisions of the Clayton Act of 1914, presumably to accomplish this, had failed. The Norris-La Guardia Act of 1932, after four decades of agitation, finally succeeded in stopping Courts from issuing injunctions to uphold yellow-dog contracts and to prevent work stoppages and the joining of trade unions, among other things.

✓   ✓   ✓

AN ACT to amend the Judicial Code and to define and limit the jurisdiction of courts sitting in equity, and for other purposes.

Be it enacted by the Senate and House of Representatives of the United States of America in Congress assembled, That no court of the United States, as herein defined, shall have jurisdiction to issue any restraining order or temporary or permanent injunction in a case involving or growing out of a labor dispute, except in a strict conformity with the provisions of this Act; nor shall any such restraining order or temporary or permanent injunction be issued contrary to the public policy declared in this Act.

SEC. 2. In the interpretation of this Act and in determining the jurisdiction and authority of the courts of the United States, as such jurisdiction and authority are herein defined and limited, the public policy of the United States is hereby declared as follows:

Whereas under prevailing economic conditions, developed with the aid of governmental authority for owners of property to organize in the corporate and other forms of ownership association, the individual unorganized worker is commonly helpless to exercise actual liberty of contract and to protect his freedom of labor, and thereby to obtain acceptable terms and conditions of employment, wherefore, though he should be free to decline to associate with his fellows, it is necessary that he have full freedom of association, self-organization, and designation of representatives of his own choosing, to negotiate the terms and conditions of his employment, and that he shall be free from the interference, restraint, or coercion of employers of labor, or their agents, in the designation of such representatives or in self-organization or in other concerted activities for the purpose of collective bargaining or other mutual aid or protection; therefore, the following definitions of, and limitations upon, the jurisdiction and authority of the courts of the the United States are hereby enacted.

SEC. 3. Any undertaking or promise, such as is described in this section, or any other undertaking or promise in conflict with the public policy declared in section 2 of this Act, is hereby declared to be contrary to the public policy of the United States, shall not be enforceable in any court of the United States and shall not afford any basis for the granting of legal or equitable relief by any such court, including specifically the following:

Every undertaking or promise hereafter made, whether written or oral, express or implied, constituting or contained in any contract or agreement of hiring or employment between any individual, firm, company, association, or corporation, and any employee or prospective employee of the same, whereby

(a) Either party to such contract or agreement undertakes or promises not to join, become, or remain a member of any labor organization or of any employer organization; or

(b) Either party to such contract or agreement undertakes or promises that he will withdraw from an employment relation in the event that he joins, becomes, or remains a member of any labor organization or of any employer organization.

SEC. 4. No court of the United States shall have jurisdiction to issue any restraining order or temporary or permanent injunction in any case involving or growing out of any labor dispute to prohibit any person or persons participating or interested in such dispute (as these terms are herein defined) from doing, whether singly or in concert, any of the following acts:

(a) Ceasing or refusing to perform any work or to remain in any relation of employment;

(b) Becoming or remaining a member of any labor organization or of any employer organization, regardless of any such undertaking or promise as is described in section 3 of this Act;

(c) Paying or giving to, or withholding from, any person participating or interested in such labor dispute, any strike or unemployment benefits or insurance, or other moneys or things of value;

(d) By all lawful means aiding any person participating or interested in any labor dispute who is being proceeded against in, or is prosecuting, any action or suit in any court of the United States or of any State;

(e) Giving publicity to the existence of, or the facts involved in, any labor dispute, whether by advertising, speaking, patrolling, or by any other method not involving fraud or violence;

(f) Assembling peaceably to act or to organize to act in promotion of their interests in a labor dispute;

(g) Advising or notifying any person of an intention to do any of the acts heretofore specified;

(h) Agreeing with other persons to do or not to do any of the acts heretofore specified; and

(i) Advising, urging, or otherwise causing or inducing without fraud or violence the acts heretofore specified, regardless of any such undertaking or promise as is described in section 3 of this Act.

SEC. 5. No court of the United States shall have jurisdiction to issue a restraining order or temporary or permanent injunction upon the ground that any of the persons participating or interested in a labor dispute constitute or are engaged in an unlawful combination or conspiracy because of the doing in concert of the acts enumerated in section 4 of this Act.

SEC. 6. No officer or member of any association or organization, and no association or organization participating or interested in a labor dispute, shall be held responsible or liable in any court of the United States for the unlawful acts of individual officers, members, or agents, except upon clear proof of actual participation in, or actual authorization of, such acts, or of ratification of such acts after actual knowledge thereof.

SEC. 7. No court of the United States shall have jurisdiction to issue a temporary or permanent injunction in any case involving or growing out of a labor dispute, as herein defined, except after hearing the testimony of witnesses in open court (with opportunity for cross-examination) in support of the allegations of a complaint made under oath, and testimony in opposition thereto, if offered, and except after findings of fact by the court, to the effect—

(a) That unlawful acts have been threatened and will be committed unless restrained or have been committed and will be continued unless restrained, but no injunction or temporary restraining order shall be issued on account of any threat or unlawful act excepting against the person or persons, association, or organization making the threat or committing the unlawful act or actually authorizing or ratifying the same after actual knowledge thereof;

(b) That substantial and irreparable injury to complainant's property will follow;

(c) That as to each item of relief granted greater injury will be inflicted upon complainant by the denial of relief than will be inflicted upon defendants by the granting of relief;

(d) That complainant has no adequate remedy at law; and

(e) That the public officers charged with the duty to protect complainant's property are unable or unwilling to furnish adequate protection.

Such hearing shall be held after due and personal notice thereof has been given, in such manner as the court shall direct, to all known persons against whom relief is sought, and also to the chief of those public officials of the county and city within which the unlawful acts have been threatened or committed charged with the duty to protect complainant's property: *Provided, however,* That if a complainant shall also allege that, unless a temporary restraining order shall be issued without notice, a substantial and irreparable injury to complainant's property will be unavoidable, such a temporary restraining order may be issued upon testimony under oath, sufficient, if sustained, to justify the court in issuing a temporary injunction upon a hearing after notice. Such a temporary restraining order shall be effective for no longer than five days and shall become void at the expiration of said five days. . . .

Sec. 9. No restraining order or temporary or permanent injunction shall be granted in a case involving or growing

out of a labor dispute, except on the basis of findings of
fact made and filed by the court in the record of the case
prior to the issuance of such restraining order or injunction; and every restraining order or injunction granted in
a case involving or growing out of a labor dispute shall
include only a prohibition of such specific act or acts as
may be expressly complained of in the bill of complaint or
petition filed in such case and as shall be expressly included in said findings of fact made and filed by the court
as provided herein. . . .

SEC. 11. In all cases arising under this Act in which a
person shall be charged with contempt in a court of the
United States (as herein defined), the accused shall enjoy
the right to a speedy and public trial by an impartial jury
of the State and district wherein the contempt shall have
been committed: *Provided,* That this right shall not apply
to contempts committed in the presence of the court or so
near thereto as to interfere directly with the administration
of justice or to apply to the misbehavior, misconduct, or
disobedience of any officer of the court in respect to the
writs, orders, or process of the court.

SEC. 12. The defendant in any proceeding for contempt
of court may file with the court a demand for the retirement of the judge sitting in the proceeding, if the contempt
arises from an attack upon the character or conduct of such
judge and if the attack occurred elsewhere than in the
presence of the court or so near thereto as to interfere
directly with the administration of justice. Upon the filing
of any such demand the judge shall thereupon proceed no
further, but another judge shall be designated in the same
manner as is provided by law. The demand shall be filed
prior to the hearing in the contempt proceeding.

THE AGRICULTURAL ADJUSTMENT ACT OF MAY 12, 1933[12]

The first New Deal Congress passed the Agricultural Adjustment Act as the first piece of important reform legislation. It did not succeed in its grand intention, for production on limited acreage simply became more intensified. On January 6, 1936, the Supreme Court found the law unconstitutional because, by taxing processors, Congress was invading the powers reserved to the States.

✓   ✓   ✓

That the present acute economic emergency being in part the consequence of a severe and increasing disparity between the prices of agriculture and other commodities, which disparity has largely destroyed the purchasing power of farmers for industrial products . . . and has seriously impaired the agricultural assets supporting the national credit structure, it is hereby declared that these conditions . . . have affected transactions in agricultural commodities with a national public interest . . . and render imperative the immediate enactment of Title I of this Act.

DECLARATION OF POLICY

SEC. 2. It is hereby declared to be the policy of Congress—

(1) To establish and maintain such balance between the production and consumption of agricultural commodities, and such marketing conditions therefor, as will reestablish prices to farmers at a level that will give agricultural commodities a purchasing power with respect to articles that

[12] *U. S. Statutes at Large*, Vol. 48, 73rd Congress, 1st Session, Ch. 25, pp. 31-36.

farmers buy, equivalent to the purchasing power of agricultural commodities in the base period. The base period in the case of all agricultural commodities except tobacco shall be the prewar period, August 1909-July 1914. In the case of tobacco, the base period shall be the postwar period, August 1919-July 1929.

(2) To approach such equality of purchasing power by gradual correction of the present inequalities therein at as rapid a rate as is deemed feasible in view of the current consumptive demand in domestic and foreign markets.

(3) To protect the consumers' interest by readjusting farm production at such level as will not increase the percentage of the consumers' retail expenditures for agricultural commodities, or products derived therefrom, which is returned to the farmer, above the percentage which was returned to the farmer in the prewar period, August 1909-July 1914. . . .

PART 2—COMMODITY BENEFITS

GENERAL POWERS

SEC. 8. In order to effecuate* the declared policy, the Secretary of Agriculture shall have power—

(1) To provide for reduction in the acreage or reduction in the production for market, or both, of any basic agricultural commodity, through agreements with producers or by other voluntary methods, and to provide for rental or benefit payments in connection therewith or upon that part of the production of any basic agricultural commodity required for domestic consumption, in such amounts as the Secretary deems fair and reasonable, to be paid out of any moneys available for such payments. Under regulations of the Secretary of Agriculture requiring adequate facilities for the storage of any non-perishable agricultural commodity on the farm, inspection and measurement of any such commodity so stored, and the locking and sealing thereof, and such other regulations as may be prescribed by the Secretary of Agriculture for the protection of such commodity and for the marketing thereof, a reasonable percentage of any benefit payment may be advanced on any

* So in original.

such commodity so stored. In any such case, such deduction may be made from the amount of the benefit payment as the Secretary of Agriculture determines will reasonably compensate for the cost of inspection and sealing, but no deduction may be made for interest.

(2) To enter into marketing agreements with processors, associations of producers, and others engaged in the handling, in the current of interstate or foreign commerce of any agricultural commodity or product thereof, after due notice and opportunity for hearing to interested parties. The making of any such agreement shall not be held to be in violation of any of the antitrust laws of the United States, and any such agreement shall be deemed to be lawful : *Provided,* That no such agreement shall remain in force after the termination of this Act. For the purpose of carrying out any such agreement the parties thereto shall be eligible for loans from the Reconstruction Finance Corporation under section 5 of the Reconstruction Finance Corporation Act. Such loans shall not be in excess of such amounts as may be authorized by the agreements.

(3) To issue licenses permitting processors, associations of producers, and others to engage in the handling, in the current of interstate or foreign commerce, of any agricultural commodity or product thereof, or any competing commodity or product thereof. Such licenses shall be subject to such terms and conditions, not in conflict with existing Acts of Congress or regulations pursuant thereto, as may be necessary to eliminate unfair practices or charges that prevent or tend to prevent the effectuation of the declared policy and the restoration of normal economic conditions in the marketing of such commodities or products and the financing thereof. . . .

PROCESSING TAX

SEC. 9. (a) To obtain revenue for extraordinary expenses incurred by reason of the national economic emergency, there shall be levied processing taxes as hereinafter provided. When the Secretary of Agriculture determines that rental or benefit payments are to be made with respect to any basic agricultural commodity, he shall proclaim such determination, and a processing tax shall be in effect with respect to such commodity from the beginning of the marketing year therefor next following the date of such proclamation. The processing tax shall be levied, assessed, and collected upon the first domestic processing of the commodity, whether of domestic production or imported, and shall be paid by the processor. . . . The processing tax shall be at such rate as equals the difference between the current average farm price for the commodity and the fair exchange value of the commodity. . . .

— 13 —

ABANDONMENT OF THE GOLD STANDARD, JUNE 5, 1933[13]

The full circle to the monetary debate, ironically, was turned in 1933 when the New Deal decided to abandon the gold standard. The Joint Resolution of June 5, 1933, did so; and the President was permitted to revalue gold (he did so at the price of $35 an ounce) and allow the Treasury to buy all gold offered at that price. By July, 1940, the Federal government controlled 80 per cent of the world's gold stocks. Very little of this had any real effect on prices —much to the New Deal's deep disappointment.

✓   ✓   ✓

JOINT RESOLUTION

To assure uniform value to the coins and currencies of the United States.

Whereas the holding of or dealing in gold affect the public interest, and are therefore subject to proper regulation and restriction; and

[13] *U. S. Statutes at Large,* Vol. 48, 78th Congress, 1st Session, Ch. 48, pp. 112-113.

Whereas the existing emergency has disclosed that provisions of obligations which purport to give the obligee a right to require payment in gold or a particular kind of coin or currency of the United States, or in an amount in money of the United States measured thereby, obstruct the power of the Congress to regulate the value of the money of the United States, and are inconsistent with the declared policy of the Congress to maintain at all times the equal power of every dollar, coined or issued by the United States, in the markets and in the payment of debts. Now, therefore, be it

Resolved by the Senate and House of Representatives of the United States of America in Congress assembled, That (a) every provision contained in or made with respect to any obligation which purports to give the obligee a right to require payment in gold or a particular kind of coin or currency, or in an amount in money of the United States measured thereby, is declared to be against public policy; and no such provision shall be contained in or made with respect to any obligation hereafter incurred. Every obligation, heretofore or hereafter incurred, whether or not any such provision is contained therein or made with respect thereto, shall be discharged upon payment, dollar for dollar, in any coin or currency which at the time of payment is legal tender for public and private debts. Any such provision contained in any law authorizing obligations to be issued by or under authority of the United States, is hereby repealed, but the repeal of any such provision shall not invalidate any other provision or authority contained in such law.

(b) As used in this resolution, the term "obligation" means an obligation (including every obligation of and to the United States, excepting currency) payable in money of the United States; and the term "coin or currency" means coin or currency of the United States, including Federal Reserve notes and circulating notes of Federal Reserve banks and national banking associations.

SEC. 2. The last sentence of paragraph (1) of subsection (b) of section 43 of the Act entitled "An Act to relieve the existing national economic emergency by increasing agricultural purchasing power, to raise revenue for extraordinary expenses incurred by reason of such emergency, to provide emergency relief with respect to agricultural indebtedness, to provide for the orderly liquidation of joint-stock land banks, and for other purposes," approved May 12, 1933, is amended to read as follows:

"All coins and currencies of the United States (including Federal Reserve notes and circulating notes of Federal Reserve banks and national banking associations) heretofore or hereafter coined or issued, shall be legal tender for all debts, public and private, public charges, taxes, duties, and dues, except that gold coins, when below the standard weight and limit of tolerance provided by law for the single piece, shall be legal tender only at valuation in proportion to their actual weight."

— 14 —

THE NATIONAL INDUSTRIAL RECOVERY ACT OF JUNE 16, 1933 [14]

Nothing displayed better the boldness—and the willingness to improvise—of the early New Deal than the writing of the National Industrial Recovery Act. To rehabilitate industry (and presumably to reestablish competition), President Roosevelt and his advisers proceeded in effect to create national industrial syndicates which, had they been permitted to function, would really have fastened monopoly practices upon the United States. On May 27, 1935, the Supreme Court, in Schechter Poultry Corporation v. United States (295 U. S. 495), in a unanimous decision declared the law unconstitutional—long after it had demonstrated its own futility. Section 7 (a) of the Act sought to

[14] *U. S. Statutes at Large,* Vol. 48, 73rd Congress, 1st Session, Ch. 90, pp. 195-198.

*give labor the right to bargain collectively; and when it
went out with the law Congress had to pass the National
Labor Relations Act in 1935.*

✓   ✓   ✓

AN ACT

To encourge national industrial recovery, to foster fair
competition, and to provide for the construction of certain useful public works, and for other purposes.

*Be it enacted by the Senate and House of Representa-
tives of the United States of America in Congress assembled,*

TITLE I—INDUSTRIAL RECOVERY

DECLARATION OF POLICY

SECTION 1. A national emergency productive of widespread unemployment and disorganization of industry,
which burdens interstate and foreign commerce, affects the
public welfare, and undermines the standards of living of
the American people, is hereby declared to exist. It is
hereby declared to be the policy of Congress to remove
obstructions to the free flow of interstate and foreign commerce which tend to diminish the amount thereof; and to
provide for the general welfare by promoting the organization of industry for the purpose of cooperative action
among trade groups, to induce and maintain united action
of labor and management under adequate governmental
sanctions and supervision, to eliminate unfair competitive
practices, to promote the fullest possible utilization of the
present productive capacity of industries, to avoid undue
restriction of production (except as may be temporarily
required), to increase the consumption of industrial and
agricultural products by increasing purchasing power, to
reduce and relieve unemployment, to improve standards of
labor, and otherwise to rehabilitate industry and to con-
serve natural resources.

ADMINISTRATIVE AGENCIES

SEC. 2. (b) The President may delegate any of his
functions and powers under this title to such officers,

agents, and employees as he may designate or appoint, and may establish an industrial planning and research agency to aid in carrying out his functions under this title. . . .

CODES OF FAIR COMPETITION

SEC. 3. (a) Upon the application to the President by one or more trade or industrial associations or groups, the President may approve a code or codes of fair competition for the trade or industry or subdivision thereof, represented by the applicant or applicants, if the President finds (1) that such associations or groups impose no inequitable restrictions on admission to membership therein and are truly representative of such trades or industries or subdivisions thereof, and (2) that such code or codes are not designed to promote monopolies or to eliminate or oppress small enterprises and will not operate to discriminate against them, and will tend to effectuate the policy of this title: . . .

(b) After the President shall have approved any such code, the provisions of such code shall be the standards of fair competition for such trade or industry or subdivision thereof. Any violation of such standards in any transaction in or affecting interstate or foreign commerce shall be deemed an unfair method of competition in commerce within the meaning of the Federal Trade Commission Act, as amended; but nothing in this title shall be construed to impair the powers of the Federal Trade Commission under such Act, as amended. . . .

(d) Upon his own motion, or if complaint is made to the President that abuses inimical to the public interest and contrary to the policy herein declared are prevalent in any trade or industry or subdivision thereof, and if no code of fair competition therefor has theretofore been approved by the President, the President, after such public notice and hearing as he shall specify, may prescribe and approve a code of fair competition for such trade or industry or subdivision thereof, which shall have the same effect as a code of fair competition approved by the President under subsection (a) of this section.

(f) When a code of fair competition has been approved or prescribed by the President under this title, any violation of any provision thereof in any transaction in or af-

fecting interstate or foreign commerce shall be a misde-
meanor and upon conviction thereof an offender shall be
fined not more than $500 for each offense, and each day
such violation continues shall be deemed a separate offense.

AGREEMENTS AND LICENSES

SEC. 4. (a) The President is authorized to enter into
agreements with, and to approve voluntary agreements
between and among, persons engaged in a trade or industry, labor organizations, and trade or industrial organizations, associations, or groups, relating to any trade or
industry, if in his judgment such agreements will aid in
effectuating the policy of this title with respect to transactions in or affecting interstate or foreign commerce, and
will be consistent with the requirements of clause (2) of
subsection (a) of section 3 for a code of fair competition.

(b) Whenever the President shall find that destructive
wage or price cutting or other activities contrary to the
policy of this title are being practiced in any trade or industry or any subdivision thereof, and, after such public
notice and hearing as he shall specify, shall find it essential
to license business enterprises in order to make effective a
code of fair competition or an agreement under this title or
otherwise to effectuate the policy of this title, and shall
publicly so announce, no person shall, after a date fixed
in such announcement, engage in or carry on any business,
in or affecting interstate or foreign commerce, specified
in such announcement, unless he shall have first obtained a
license issued pursuant to such regulations as the President
shall prescribe. The President may suspend or revoke any
such license, after due notice and opportunity for hearing,
for violations of the terms or conditions thereof. Any order
of the President suspending or revoking any such license
shall be final if in accordance with law. Any person who,
without such a license or in violation of any condition
thereof, carries on any such business for which a license
is so required, shall, upon conviction thereof, be fined not
more than $500, or imprisoned not more than six months,
or both, and each day such violation continues shall be
deemed a separate offense. Notwithstanding the provisions
of section 2 (c), this subsection shall cease to be in effect
at the expiration of one year after the date of enactment

of this Act or sooner if the President shall by proclamation or the Congress shall by joint resolution declare that the emergency recognized by section 1 has ended.

SEC. 5. While this title is in effect (or in the case of a license, while section 4 (a) is in effect) and for sixty days thereafter, any code, agreement, or license approved, prescribed, or issued and in effect under this title, and any action complying with the provisions thereof taken during such period, shall be exempt from the provisions of the antitrust laws of the United States. . . .

SEC. 7. (a) Every code of fair competition, agreement, and license approved, prescribed, or issued under this title shall contain the following conditions: (1) That employees shall have the right to organize and bargain collectively through representatives of their own choosing, and shall be free from the interference, restraint, or coercion of employers of labor, or their agents, in the designation of such representatives or in self-organization or in other concerted activities for the purpose of collective bargaining or other mutual aid or protection: (2) that no employee and no one seeking employment shall be required as a condition of employment to join any company union or to refrain from joining, organizing, or assisting a labor organization of his own choosing; and (3) that employers shall comply with the maximum hours of labor, minimum rates of pay, and other conditions of employment, approved or prescribed by the President.

— 15 —

THE RECIPROCAL TRADE AGREEMENTS ACT OF JUNE 12, 1934[15]

In 1934, the United States Congress took a revolutionary step: it placed the power of tariff-making in the hands of the President. He was authorized to make reciprocal trade agreements with other countries by which prevailing duties could be cut by as much as 50 per cent. Between 1934 and 1941, the Secretary of State negotiated some 26 such agreements, and at least two-thirds of American foreign trade was affected. The Act was renewed regularly in Congress (although the permissible period was cut subsequently from three years to one) and continues on the statute books—with changes, of course, from time to time.

✦   ✦   ✦

AN ACT

To amend the Tariff Act of 1930.

Be it enacted by the Senate and House of Representatives of the United States of America in Congress assembled, That the Tariff Act of 1930 is amended by adding at the end of title III the following:

PART III—PROMOTION OF FOREIGN TRADE

"SEC. 350. (a) For the purpose of expanding foreign markets for the products of the United States (as a means of assisting in the present emergency in restoring the American standard of living, in overcoming domestic unemployment and the present economic depression, in increasing the purchasing power of the American public,

[15] *U. S. Statutes at Large,* Vol. 48, 73rd Congress, 2nd Session, Ch. 474, pp. 943-945.

and in establishing and maintaining a better relationship among various branches of American agriculture, industry, mining, and commerce) by regulating the admission of foreign goods into the United States in accordance with the characteristics and needs of various branches of American production so that foreign markets will be made available to those branches of American production which require and are capable of developing such outlets by affording corresponding market opportunities for foreign products in the United States, the President, whenever he finds as a fact that any existing duties or other import restrictions of the United States or any foreign country are unduly burdening and restricting the foreign trade of the United States and that the purpose above declared will be promoted by the means hereinafter specified, is authorized from time to time—

"(1) To enter into foreign trade agreements with foreign governments or instrumentalities thereof; and

"(2) To proclaim such modifications of existing duties and other import restrictions, or such additional import restrictions, or such continuance, and for such minimum periods, of existing customs or excise treatment of any article covered by foreign trade agreements, as are required or appropriate to carry out any foreign trade agreement that the President has entered into hereunder. No proclamation shall be made increasing or decreasing by more than 50 per centum any existing rate of duty or transferring any article between the dutiable and free lists. The proclaimed duties and other import restrictions shall apply to articles the growth, produce, or manufacture of all foreign countries, whether imported directly, or indirectly: *Provided,* That the President may suspend the application to articles the growth, produce, or manufacture of any country because of its discriminatory treatment of American commerce or because of other acts or policies which in his opinion tend to defeat the purposes set forth in this section; and the proclaimed duties and other import restrictions shall be in effect from and after such time as is specified in the proclamation. The President may at any time terminate any such proclamation in whole or in part.

"(b) Nothing in this section shall be construed to prevent the application, with respect to rates of duty established under this section pursuant to agreements with countries other than Cuba, of the provisions of the treaty of commercial reciprocity concluded between the United States and the Republic of Cuba on December 11, 1902, or to preclude giving effect to an exclusive agreement with Cuba concluded under this section, modifying the existing preferential customs treatment of any article the growth, produce, or manufacture of Cuba: *Provided,* That the duties payable on such an article shall in no case be increased or decreased by more than 50 per centum of the duties now payable thereon.

"(c) As used in this section, the term 'duties and other import restrictions' includes (1) rate and form of import duties and classification of articles, and (2) limitations, prohibitions, charges, and exactions other than duties, imposed on importation or imposed for the regulation of imports." . . .

SEC. 2. (b) Every foreign trade agreement concluded pursuant to this Act shall be subject to termination, upon due notice to the foreign government concerned, at the end of not more than three years from the date on which the agreement comes into force, and, if not then terminated, shall be subject to termination thereafter upon not more than six months' notice.

(c) The authority of the President to enter into foreign trade agreements under section 1 of this Act shall terminate on the expiration of three years from the date of the enactment of this Act.

SEC. 3. Nothing in this Act shall be construed to give any authority to cancel or reduce, in any manner, any of the indebtedness of any foreign country to the United States.

SEC. 4. Before any foreign trade agreement is concluded with any foreign government or instrumentality thereof under the provisions of this Act, reasonable public notice of the intention to negotiate an agreement with such government or instrumentality shall be given in order that any interested person may have an opportunity to present his views to the President, or to such agency as the President may designate, under such rules and regulations as the President may prescribe; and before concluding such agreement the President shall seek information and advice with respect thereto from the United States Tariff Commission, the Departments of State, Agriculture, and Commerce and from such other sources as he may deem appropriate.

— 16 —

THE SECURITIES EXCHANGE ACT OF JUNE 6, 1934 [16]

One of the notable accomplishments of the New Deal was the passage of the Securities Exchange Act of June 6, 1934. This law gave the Federal Reserve Board control over margin requirements on brokers' loans, outlawed specified market practices, set up machinery for regulating security exchanges, called for the publication of information about issues being traded on exchanges—and created the Securities and Exchange Commission (SEC) to administer these large powers. One of the most important was the registering of securities and the furnishing of information about the companies issuing them.

⸸   ⸸   ⸸

SEC. 2. For the reasons hereinafter enumerated transactions in securities as commonly conducted . . . are affected with a national public interest which makes it necessary to provide for regulation and control of such transactions . . . to require appropriate reports and to make such regulation and control reasonably complete and effective in order to protect interstate commerce, the national credit . . . to protect and make more effective the national banking system and Federal Reserve System, and

[16] *U. S. Statutes at Large,* Vol. 48, 73rd Congress, 2nd Session, Ch. 404, pp. 882-895.

to insure the maintenance of fair and honest markets in such transactions:

(1) Such transactions (a) are carried on in large volume by the public generally and in large part originate outside the States in which the exchanges and over-the-counter markets are located and/or are affected by means of the mails and instrumentalities of interstate commerce; (b) constitute an important part of the current of interstate commerce; (c) involve in large part the securities of issuers engaged in interstate commerce; (d) involve the use of credit, directly affect the financing of trade, industry, and transportation in interstate commerce, and directly affect and influence the volume of interstate commerce; and affect the national credit.

(2) The prices established and offered in such transactions are generally disseminated and quoted throughout the United States and foreign countries and constitute a basis for determining and establishing the prices at which securities are bought and sold, the amount of certain taxes owing to the United States and to the several States by owners, buyers, and sellers of securities, and the value of collateral for bank loans.

(3) Frequently the prices of securities on such exchanges and markets are susceptible to manipulation and control, and the dissemination of such prices gives rise to excessive speculation, resulting in sudden and unreasonable fluctuations in the prices of securities which (a) cause alternately unreasonable expansion and unreasonable contraction of the volume of credit available for trade, transportation, and industry in interstate commerce, (b) hinder the proper appraisal of the value of securities and thus prevent a fair calculation of taxes owing to the United States and to the several States by owners, buyers, and sellers of securities, and (c) prevent the fair valuation of collateral for bank loans and/or obstruct the effective operation of the national banking system and Federal Reserve System.

(4) National emergencies, which produce widespread unemployment and the dislocation of trade, transportation, and industry, and which burden interstate commerce and adversely affect the general welfare, are precipitated, intensified, and prolonged by manipulation and sudden and

unreasonable fluctuations of security prices and by excessive speculation on such exchanges and markets, and to meet such emergencies the Federal Government is put to such great expense as to burden the national credit. . . .

SECURITIES AND EXCHANGE COMMISSION

SEC. 4. (a) There is hereby established a Securities and Exchange Commission (hereinafter referred to as the "Commission") to be composed of five commissioners to be appointed by the President by and with the advice and consent of the Senate. Not more than three of such commissioners shall be members of the same political party, and in making appointments members of different political parties shall be appointed alternately as nearly as may be practicable. No commissioner shall engage in any other business, vocation, or employment than that of serving as commissioner, nor shall any commissioner participate, directly or indirectly, in any stock-market operations or transactions of a character subject to regulation by the Commission pursuant to this title. . . .

TRANSACTIONS ON UNREGISTERED EXCHANGES

SEC. 5. It shall be unlawful for any broker, dealer, or exchange, directly or indirectly, to make use of the mails or any means or instrumentality of interstate commerce for the purpose of using any facility of an exchange within or subject to the jurisdiction of the United States to effect any transaction in a security, or to report any such transaction, unless such exchange (1) is registered as a national securities exchange under section 6 of this title, or (2) is exempted from such registration upon application by the exchange because, in the opinion of the Commission, by reason of the limited volume of transactions effected on such exchange, it is not practicable and not necessary or appropriate in the public interest or for the protection of investors to require such registration.

REGISTRATION OF NATIONAL SECURITIES EXCHANGES

SEC. 6. (a) Any exchange may be registered with the Commission as a national securities exchange under the terms and conditions hereinafter provided in this section, by filing a registration statement in such form as the Commission may prescribe . . .

REGISTRATION REQUIREMENTS FOR SECURITIES

SEC. 12. (a) It shall be unlawful for any member, broker, or dealer to effect any transaction in any security (other than an exempted security) on a national securities exchange unless a registration is effective as to such security for such exchange in accordance with the provisions of this title and the rules and regulations thereunder.

(b) A security may be registered on a national securities exchange by the issuer filing an application with the exchange (and filing with the Commission such duplicate originals thereof as the Commission may require), which application shall contain—

(1) Such information, in such detail, as to the issuer and any person directly or indirectly controlling or controlled by, or under direct or indirect common control with, the issuer, and any guarantor of the security as to principal or interest or both, as the Commission may by rules and regulations require, as necessary or appropriate in the public interest or for the protection of investors, in respect of the following:

(A) the organization, financial structure and nature of the business;

(B) the terms, position, rights, and privileges of the different classes of securities outstanding;

(C) the terms on which their securities are to be, and during the preceding three years have been, offered to the public or otherwise;

(D) the directors, officers, and underwriters, and each security holder of record holding more than 10 per centum of any class of any equity security of the issuer (other than an exempted security), their remuneration and their interests in the securities of, and their material contracts with, the issuer and any person directly or indirectly controlling or controlled by, or under direct or indirect common control with, the issuer;

(E) remuneration to others than directors and officers exceeding $20,000 per annum;

(F) bonus and profit-sharing arrangements;

(G) management and service contracts;

(H) options existing or to be created in respect of their securities;

(I) balance sheets for not more than the three preceding fiscal years, certified if required by the rules and regulations of the Commission by independent public accountants;

(J) profit and loss statements for not more than the three preceding fiscal years, certified if required by the rules and regulations of the Commission by independent public accountants; and

(K) any further financial statements which the Commission may deem necessary or appropriate for the protection of investors. . . .

PERIODICAL AND OTHER REPORTS

SEC. 13. (a) Every issuer of a security registered on a national securities exchange shall file the information, documents, and reports below specified with the exchange (and shall file with the Commission such duplicate originals thereof as the Commission may require), in accordance with such rules and regulations as the Commission may prescribe as necessary or appropriate for the proper protection of investors and to insure fair dealing in the security—

(1) Such information and documents as the Commission may require to keep reasonably current the information and documents filed pursuant to section 12.

(2) Such annual reports, certified if required by the rules and regulations of the Commission by independent public accountants, and such quarterly reports, as the Commission may prescribe.

(b) The Commission may prescribe, in regard to reports made pursuant to this title, the form or forms in which the required information shall be set forth, the items or details to be shown in the balance sheet and the earning statement, and the methods to be followed in the preparation of reports, in the appraisal or valuation of assets and liabilities, in the determination of depreciation and depletion, in the differentiation of recurring and nonrecurring income, in the differentiation of investment and operating income, and in the preparation, where the

Commission deems it necessary or desirable, of separate and/or consolidated balance sheets or income accounts of any person directly or indirectly controlling or controlled by the issuer, or any person under direct or indirect common control with the issuer; but in the case of the reports of any person whose methods of accounting are prescribed under the provisions of any law of the United States, or any rule or regulation thereunder, the rules and regulations of the Commission with respect to reports shall not be inconsistent with the requirements imposed by such law or rule or regulation in respect of the same subject matter, and, in the case of carriers subject to the provisions of section 20 of the Interstate Commerce Act, as amended, or carriers required pursuant to any other Act of Congress to make reports of the same general character as those required under such section 20, shall permit such carriers to file with the Commission and the exchange duplicate copies of the reports and other documents filed with the Interstate Commerce Commission, or with the governmental authority administering such other Act of Congress, in lieu of the reports, information and documents required under this section and section 12 in respect of the same subject matter.

(c) If in the judgment of the Commission any report required under subsection (a) is inapplicable to any specified class or classes of issuers, the Commission shall require in lieu thereof of the submission of such reports of comparable character as it may deem applicable to such class or classes of issuers. . . .

— 17 —

THE NATIONAL LABOR RELATIONS ACT OF JULY 3 AND JULY 5, 1935 [17]

The New Deal tried again and again to accord labor full rights to organize and to bargain collectively through its own representatives. It did so in Section 7 (a) of the National Industrial Recovery Act of 1933; the creation of the National Labor Board in 1933; and that of the National Labor Relations Board of 1934. None of these worked; the upshot was the decision to write in effect a whole code of labor in 1935. This arose out of Senator Robert F. Wagner's attempt to outlaw company unions and compel the recognition of collective bargaining in 1934. He fathered the new bill, and it is associated with his name.

✦ ✦ ✦

AN ACT

To diminish the causes of labor disputes burdening or obstructing interstate and foreign commerce, to create a National Labor Relations Board, and for other purposes.

Be it enacted by the Senate and House of Representatives of the United States of America in Congress assembled,

FINDINGS AND POLICY

SECTION 1. The denial by employers of the right of employees to organize and the refusal by employers to accept the procedure of collective bargaining lead to strikes and

[17] *U. S. Statutes at Large,* Vol. 49, 74th Congress, 1st Session, Ch. 372, pp. 449-455.

other forms of industrial strife or unrest, which have the intent or the necessary effect of burdening or obstructing commerce by (a) impairing the efficiency, safety, or operation of the instrumentalities of commerce; (b) occurring in the current of commerce; (c) materially affecting, restraining, or controlling the flow of raw materials or manufactured or processed goods from or into the channels of commerce, or the prices of such materials or goods in commerce; or (d) causing diminution of employment and wages in such volume as substantially to impair or disrupt the market for goods flowing from or into the channels of commerce.

The inequality of bargaining power between employees who do not possess full freedom of association or actual liberty of contract, and employers who are organized in the corporate or other forms of ownership association substantially burdens and affects the flow of commerce, and tends to aggravate recurrent business depressions, by depressing wage rates and the purchasing power of wage earners in industry and by preventing the stabilization of competitive wage rates and working conditions within and between industries.

Experience has proved that protection by law of the right of employees to organize and bargain collectively safeguards commerce from injury, impairment, or interruption, and promotes the flow of commerce by removing certain recognized sources of industrial strife and unrest, by encouraging practices fundamental to the friendly adjustment of industrial disputes arising out of differences as to wages, hours, or other working conditions, and by restoring equality of bargaining power between employers and employees.

It is hereby declared to be the policy of the United States to eliminate the causes of certain substantial obstructions to the free flow of commerce and to mitigate and eliminate these obstructions when they have occurred by encouraging the practice and procedure of collective bargaining and by protecting the exercise by workers of full freedom of association, self-organization, and designation of representatives of their own choosing, for the purpose of negotiating the terms and conditions of their employment or other mutual aid or protection. . . .

RIGHTS OF EMPLOYEES

SEC. 7. Employees shall have the right to self-organization, to form, join, or assist labor organizations, to bargain collectively through representatives of their own choosing, and to engage in concerted activities, for the purpose of collective bargaining or other mutual aid or protection.

SEC. 8. It shall be an unfair labor practice for an employer—

(1) To interfere with, restrain, or coerce employees in the exercise of the rights guaranteed in section 7.

(2) To dominate or interfere with the formation or administration of any labor organization or contribute financial or other support to it: *Provided,* That subject to rules and regulations made and published by the Board pursuant to section 6 (a), an employer shall not be prohibited from permitting employees to confer with him during working hours without loss of time or pay.

(3) By discrimination in regard to hire or tenure of employment or any term or condition of employment to encourage or discourage membership in any labor organization: *Provided,* That nothing in this Act, or in the National Industrial Recovery Act (U. S. C., Supp. VII, title 15, secs. 701-712), as amended from time to time, or in any code or agreement approved or prescribed thereunder, or in any other statute of the United States, shall preclude an employer from making an agreement with a labor organization (not established, maintained, or assisted by any action defined in this Act as an unfair labor practice) to require as a condition of employment membership therein, if such labor organization is the representative of the employees as provided in section 9 (a), in the appropriate collective bargaining unit covered by such agreement when made.

(4) To discharge or otherwise discriminate against an employee because he has filed charges or given testimony under this Act.

(5) To refuse to bargain collectively with the representatives of his employees, subject to the provisions of Section 9 (a).

REPRESENTATIVES AND ELECTIONS

SEC. 9. (a) Representatives designated or selected for the purposes of collective bargaining by the majority of the employees in a unit appropriate for such purposes, shall be the exclusive representatives of all the employees in such unit for the purposes of collective bargaining in respect to rates of pay, wages, hours of employment, or other conditions of employment: *Provided,* That any individual employee or a group of employees shall have the right at any time to present grievances to their employer.

(b) The Board shall decide in each case whether, in order to insure to employees the full benefit of their right to self-organization and to collective bargaining, and otherwise to effectuate the policies of this Act, the unit appropriate for the purposes of collective bargaining shall be the employer unit, craft unit, plant unit, or subdivision thereof.

(c) Whenever a question affecting commerce arises concerning the representation of employees, the Board may investigate such controversy and certify to the parties, in writing, the name or names of the representatives that have been designated or selected. In any such investigation, the Board shall provide for an appropriate hearing upon due notice, either in conjunction with a proceeding under section 10 or otherwise, and may take a secret ballot of employees, or utilize any other suitable method to as-ascertin* such representatives.

(d) Whenever an order of the Board made pursuant to section 10 (c) is based in whole or in part upon facts certified following an investigation pursuant to subsection (c) of this section, and there is a petition for the enforcement or review of such order, such certification and the record of such investigation shall be included in the transcript of the entire record required to be filed under subsections 10 (e) or 10 (f), and thereupon the decree of the court enforcing, modifying, or setting aside in whole or in part the order of the Board shall be made and entered upon the pleadings, testimony, and proceedings set forth in such transcript.

* So in original.

PREVENTION OF UNFAIR LABOR PRACTICES

SEC. 10. (a) The Board is empowered, as hereinafter provided, to prevent any person from engaging in any unfair labor practice (listed in section 8) affecting commerce. This power shall be exclusive, and shall not be affected by any other means of adjustment or prevention that has been or may be established by agreement, code, law, or otherwise.

(b) Whenever it is charged that any person has engaged in or is engaging in any such unfair labor practice, the Board, or any agent or agency designated by the Board for such purposes, shall have power to issue and cause to be served upon such person a complaint stating the charges in that respect, and containing a notice of hearing before the Board or a member thereof, or before a designated agent or agency, at a place therein fixed, not less than five days after the serving of said complaint. Any such complaint may be amended by the member, agent, or agency conducting the hearing or the Board in its discretion at any time prior to the issuance of an order based thereon. The person so complained of shall have the right to file an answer to the original or amended complaint and to appear in person or otherwise and give testimony at the place and time fixed in the complaint./In the discretion of the member, agent or agency conducting the hearing or the Board, any other person may be allowed to intervene in the said proceeding and to present testimony. In any such proceeding the rules of evidence prevailing in courts of law or equity shall not be controlling. . . .

(f) Any person aggrieved by a final order of the Board granting or denying in whole or in part the relief sought may obtain a review of such order in any circuit court of appeals of the United States in the circuit wherein the unfair labor practice in question was alleged to have been engaged in or wherein such person resides or transacts business, or in the Court of Appeals of the District of Columbia, by filing in such court a written petition praying that the order of the Board be modified or set aside. A copy of such petition shall be forthwith served upon the Board, and thereupon the aggrieved party shall file in the court a transcript of the entire record in the proceeding, certified by the Board, including the pleading and testimony upon which the order complained of was entered and the findings and order of the Board. Upon such filing, the court shall proceed in the same manner as in the case of an applicaton by the Board under subsection (e), and shall have the same exclusive jurisdiction to grant to the Board such temporary relief or restraining order as it deems just and proper, and in like manner to make and enter a decree enforcing, modifying, and enforcing as so modified, or setting aside in whole or in part the order of the Board; and the findings of the Board as to the facts, if supported by evidence, shall in like manner be conclusive. . . .

— 18 —

THE SOCIAL SECURITY ACT OF AUGUST 14, 1935 [18]

One of the great accomplishments of the New Deal was the passage of the Social Security Act, also associated with the name of Senator Wagner of New York. It was a complex piece of legislation and included provisions for the aged, the unemployed, dependent children, and others. Regularly, Congress liberalized the Act as regards coverage of workers entitled to annuity payments upon retirement, and by 1960 at least 90 per cent of all those working (whether self-employed or not) and their dependents were being protected. By 1960, the tax to pay for this was up to 6 per cent and the maximum earnings on which the tax was imposed were $4,800.

✓   ✓   ✓

[18] *U. S. Statutes at Large,* Vol. 49, 74th Congress, 1st Session, Ch. 531, pp. 531-639.

An Act to provide for the general welfare by establishing a system of Federal old-age benefits, and by enabling the several States to make more adequate provision for aged persons, blind persons, dependent and crippled children, maternal and child welfare, public health and the administration of their unemployment compensation laws; to establish a Social Security Board; to raise revenue and for other purposes. . . .

TITLE II—FEDERAL OLD-AGE BENEFITS

OLD-AGE RESERVE ACCOUNT

Section 201. (a) There is hereby created an account in the Treasury of the United States to be known as the "Old-Age Reserve Account" hereinafter in this title called the "Account." There is hereby authorized to be appropriated to the Account for each fiscal year, beginning with the fiscal year ending June 30, 1937, an amount sufficient as an annual premium to provide for the payments required under this title, such amount to be determined on a reserve basis in accordance with accepted actuarial principles, and based upon such tables of mortality as the Secretary of the Treasury shall from time to time adopt, and upon an interest rate of 3 per centum per annum compounded annually. The Secretary of the Treasury shall submit annually to the Bureau of the Budget an estimate of the appropriations to be made to the Account.

(b) It shall be the duty of the Secretary of the Treasury to invest such portion of the amounts credited to the Account as is not, in his judgment, required to meet current withdrawals. Such investment may be made only in interest-bearing obligations of the United States or in obligations guaranteed as to both principal and interest by the United States. For such purpose such obligations may be acquired (1) on original issue at par, or (2) by purchase of outstanding obligations at the market price. . . .

OLD-AGE BENEFIT PAYMENTS

Sec. 202. (a) Every qualified individual (as defined in section 210) shall be entitled to receive, with respect to the period beginning on the date he attains the age of sixty-five, or on January 1, 1942, whichever is the later, and ending on the date of his death, an old-age benefit (payable as nearly as practicable in equal monthly installments) as follows:

(1) If the total wages (as defined in section 210) determined by the Board to have been paid to him, with respect to employment (as defined in section 210) after December 31, 1936, and before he attained the age of sixty-five, were not more than $3,000, the old-age benefit shall be at a monthly rate of one-half of 1 per centum of such total wages;

(2) If such total wages were more than $3,000, the old-age benefit shall be at a monthly rate equal to the sum of the following:

(A) One-half of 1 per centum of $3,000; plus

(B) One-twelfth of 1 per centum of the amount by which such total wages exceeded $3,000 and did not exceed $45,000; plus

(C) One-twenty-fourth of 1 per centum of the amount by which such total wages exceeded $45,000.

(b) In no case shall the monthly rate computed under subsection (a) exceed $85.

(c) If the Board finds at any time that more or less than the correct amount has theretofore been paid to any individual under this section, then, under regulations made by the Board, proper adjustments shall be made in connection with subsequent payments under this section to the same individual.

(d) Whenever the Board finds that any qualified individual has received wages with respect to regular employment after he attained the age of sixty-five, the old-age benefit payable to such individual shall be reduced, for each calendar month in any part of which such regular employment occurred, by an amount equal to one month's benefit. Such reduction shall be made, under regulations prescribed by the Board, by deductions from one or more payments of old-age benefit to such individual.

TITLE III—GRANTS TO STATES FOR UNEMPLOYMENT COMPENSATION ADMINISTRATION

APPROPRIATION

Section 301. For the purpose of assisting the States in the administration of their unemployment compensation laws, there is hereby authorized to be appropriated, for the fiscal year ending June 30, 1936, the sum of $4,000,000, and for each fiscal year thereafter the sum of $49,000,000, to be used as hereinafter provided. . . .

PROVISIONS OF STATE LAWS

Sec. 303. (a) The Board shall make no certification for payment to any State unless it finds that the law of such State, approved by the Board under Title IX, includes provisions for—

(1) Such methods of administration (other than those relating to selection, tenure of office, and compensation of personnel) as are found by the Board to be reasonably calculated to insure full payment of unemployment compensation when due; and

(2) Payment of unemployment compensation solely through public employment offices in the State or such other agencies as the Board may approve; and

(3) Opportunity for a fair hearing, before an impartial tribunal, for all individuals whose claims for unemployment compensation are denied; and

(4) The payment of all money received in the unemployment fund of such State, immediately upon such receipt, to the Secretary of the Treasury to the credit of the Unemployment Trust Fund established by section 904; and

(5) Expenditure of all money requisitioned by the State agency from the Unemployment Trust Fund, in the payment of unemployment compensation, exclusive of expenses of administration; and

(6) The making of such reports, in such form and containing such information, as the Board may from time to time require, and compliance with such provisions as the Board may from time to time find necessary

to assure the correctness and verification of such reports; and

(7) Making available upon request to any agency of the United States charged with the administration of public works or assistance through public employment, the name, address, ordinary occupation and employment status of each recipient of unemployment compensation, and a statement of such recipient's rights to further compensation under such law.

(b) Whenever the Board, after reasonable notice and opportunity for hearing to the State agency charged with the administration of the State law, finds that in the administration of the law there is—

(1) a denial, in a substantial number of cases, of unemployment compensation to individuals entitled thereto under such law; or

(2) a failure to comply substantially with any provision specified in subsection (a);

the Board shall notify such State agency that further payments will not be made to the State until the Board is satisfied that there is no longer any such denial or failure to comply. Until it is so satisfied it shall make no further certification to the Secretary of the Treasury with respect to such State.

TITLE IV—GRANTS TO STATES FOR AID TO DEPENDENT CHILDREN

APPROPRIATION

SECTION 401. For the purpose of enabling each State to furnish financial assistance, as far as practicable under the conditions in such State, to needy dependent children, there is hereby authorized to be appropriated for the fiscal year ending June 30, 1936, the sum of $24,750,000, and there is hereby authorized to be appropriated for each fiscal year thereafter a sum sufficient to carry out the purposes of this title. The sums made available under this section shall be used for making payments to States which have submitted, and had approved by the Board, State plans for aid to dependent children. . . .

SEC. 811. When used in this title—

(a) The term "wages" means all remuneration for employment, including the cash value of all remuneration paid in any medium other than cash; except that such term shall not include that part of the remuneration which, after remuneration equal to $3,000 has been paid to an individual by an employer with respect to employment during any calendar year, is paid to such individual by such employer with respect to employment during such calendar year.

(b) The term "employment" means any service, of whatever nature, performed within the United States by an employee for his employer, except—

(1) Agricultural labor;

(2) Domestic service in a private home;

(3) Casual labor not in the course of the employer's trade or business;

(4) Service performed by an individual who has attained the age of sixty-five;

(5) Service performed as an officer or member of the crew of a vessel documented under the laws of the United States or of any foreign country;

(6) Service performed in the employ of the United States Government or of an instrumentality of the United States;

(7) Service performed in the employ of a State, a political subdivision thereof, or an instrumentality of one or more States or political subdivisions;

(8) Service performed in the employ of a corporation, community chest, fund, or foundation, organized and operated exclusively for religious, charitable, scientific, literary, or educational purposes, or for the prevention of cruelty to children or animals, no part of the net earnings of which inures to the benefit of any private shareholder or individual.

TITLE IX—TAX ON EMPLOYERS OF EIGHT OR MORE

IMPOSITION OF TAX

SECTION 901. On and after January 1, 1936, every employer (as defined in section 907) shall pay for each calendar year an excise tax, with respect to having individuals in his employ, equal to the following percentages of the total wages (as defined in section 907) payable by him (regardless of the time of payment) with respect to employment (as defined in section 907) during such calendar year:

(1) With respect to employment during the calendar year 1936 the rate shall be 1 per centum;

(2) With respect to employment during the calendar year 1937 the rate shall be 2 per centum;

(3) With respect to employment after December 31, 1937, the rate shall be 3 per centum.

— 19 —

THE BANKING ACT OF AUGUST 23, 1935 [19]

The depression of the 1930's had revealed the many weaknesses of the American banking system. The New Deal was responsible for four enactments—the Emergency Banking Act of March 9, 1933, the Banking Act of June 16, 1933, the Federal Deposit Insurance Act of June 16, 1934, and the Banking Act of August 23, 1935. The last, in particular, centralized authority within the system itself and reorganized the Open Market Committee, shifting control over it from the reserve banks to the Board. Central banking was now fully established.

✓   ✓   ✓

[19] *U. S. Statutes at Large,* Vol. 49, 74th Congress, 1st Session, Ch. 614, pp. 704-707.

TITLE II—AMENDMENTS TO THE
FEDERAL RESERVE ACT

Hereafter the Federal Reserve Board shall be known as the "Board of Governors of the Federal Reserve System."

Any Federal Reserve bank under rules and regulations prescribed by the Board of Governors of the Federal Reserve System may make advances to any member bank on its time or demand notes having maturities of not more than four months and which are secured to the satisfaction of such Federal Reserve bank. Each such note shall bear interest at a rate not less than one-half of 1 per centum higher than the highest discount rate in effect at such Federal Reserve bank on the date of such note. . . .

SEC. 205. (a) There is hereby created a Federal Open Market Committee . . . which shall consist of the members of the Board of Governors of the Federal Reserve System and five representatives of the Federal Reserve banks to be selected as hereinafter provided. . . .

(b) No Federal Reserve bank shall engage or decline to engage in open-market operations under section 14 of this Act except in accordance with the direction of and regulations adopted by the Committee. The Committee shall consider, adopt, and transmit to the several Federal Reserve banks, regulations relating to the open-market transactions of such banks.

(c) The time, character, and volume of all purchases and sales of paper described in section 14 of this Act as eligible for open-market operations shall be governed with a view to accommodating commerce and business and with regard to their bearing upon the general credit situation of the country.

SEC. 206. (a) Subsection (b) of section 14 of the Federal Reserve Act, as amended, is amended by inserting before the semicolon at the end thereof a colon and the following: *Provided,* That any bonds, notes, or other obligations which are direct obligations of the United States or which are fully guaranteed by the United States as to principal and interest may be bought and sold without regard to maturities but only in the open market."

(b) Subsection (d) of section 14 of the Federal Reserve Act, as amended, is amended by adding at the end thereof the following: "but each such bank shall establish such rates every fourteen days, or oftener if deemed necessary by the Board."

SEC. 207. The sixth paragraph of section 19 of the Federal Reserve Act, as amended, is amended to read as follows:

"Notwithstanding the other provisions of this section, the Board of Governors of the Federal Reserve System, upon the affirmative vote of not less than four of its members, in order to prevent injurious credit expansion or contraction, may by regulation change the requirements as to reserves to be maintained against demand or time deposits or both by member banks in reserve and central reserve cities or by member banks not in reserve or central reserve cities or by all member banks; but the amount of the reserves required to be maintained by any such member bank as a result of any such change shall not be less than the amount of the reserves required by law to be maintained by such bank on the date of enactment of the Banking Act of 1935 nor more than twice such amount."

SEC. 208. The first paragraph of section 24 of the Federal Reserve Act, as amended, is amended to read as follows:

"SEC. 24. Any national banking association may make real-estate loans secured by first liens upon improved real estate, including improved farm land and improved business and residential properties. A loan secured by real estate within the meaning of this section shall be in the form of an obligation or obligations secured by mortgage, trust deed, or other such instrument upon real estate, and any national banking association may purchase any obligation so secured when the entire amount of such obligation is sold to the association. The amount of any such loan hereafter made shall not exceed 50 per centum of the appraised value of the real estate offered as security and no such loan shall be made for a longer term than five years . . . Any such association may continue hereafter as heretofore to receive time and savings deposits and to pay interest on the same, but the rate of interest which such association may pay upon such time deposits or upon sav-

ings or other deposits shall not exceed the maximum rate
authorized by law to be paid upon such deposits by State
banks or trust companies organized under the laws of the
State in which such association is located." . . .

— 20 —

THE AGRICULTURAL ADJUSTMENT ACT OF FEBRUARY 16, 1938[20]

*In February, 1936, Congress passed the Soil Conserva-
tion and Domestic Allotment Act, in another attempt to
restrict crop production. But because it failed like its
predecessor, once more Congress tried, this time in 1938.
Parity prices and parity income—set up as guide lines in
1936—were continued, coupled with the idea of the "ever-
normal granary." Payments were to be made to farmers in
the interests of soil conservation; nevertheless the surpluses continued to pile up, while farmer income was not
materially improved.*

✓   ✓   ✓

AN ACT

To provide for the conservation of national soil resources
and to provide an adequate and balanced flow of agricultural commodities in interstate and foreign commerce
and for other purposes.

*Be it enacted by the Senate and House of Representa-
tives of the United States of America in Congress assembled,* That this Act may be cited as the "Agricultural
Adjustment Act of 1938."

[20] *U. S. Statutes at Large,* Vol. 52, 75th Congress, 3rd Session,
Ch. 30, pp. 31-54.

DECLARATION OF POLICY

SEC. 2. It is hereby declared to be the policy of Congress to continue the Soil Conservation and Domestic Allotment Act, as amended, for the purpose of conserving national resources, preventing the wasteful use of soil fertility, and of preserving, maintaining, and rebuilding the farm and ranch land resources in the national public interest; to accomplish these purposes through the encouragement of soil-building and soil-conserving crops and practices; to assist in the marketing of agricultural commodities for domestic consumption and for export; and to regulate interstate and foreign commerce in cotton, wheat, corn, tobacco, and rice to the extent necessary to provide an orderly, adequate, and balanced flow of such commodities in interstate and foregin commerce through storage of reserve supplies, loans, marketing quotas, assisting farmers to obtain, insofar as practicable, parity prices for such commodities and parity of income, and assisting consumers to obtain an adequate and steady supply of such commodities at fair prices.

TITLE I—AMENDMENTS TO SOIL CONSERVATION AND DOMESTIC ALLOTMENT ACT

POWERS UNDER SOIL-CONSERVATION PROGRAM

SEC. 101. Section 8 (b) and (c) of the Soil Conservation and Domestic Allotment Act, as amended, are amended to read as follows:

"(b) Subject to the limitations provided in subsection (a) of this section, the Secretary shall have power to carry out the purposes specified in clauses (1), (2), (3), (4), and (5) of section 7 (a) by making payments or grants of other aid to agricultural producers, including tenants and sharecroppers, in amounts determined by the Secretary to be fair and reasonable in connection with the effectuation of such purposes during the year with respect to which such payments or grants are made, and measured by (1) their treatment or use of their land, or a part thereof, for soil restoration, soil conservation, or the prevention of erosion; (2) changes in the use of their land; (3) their equitable share, as determined by the Secretary, of the normal national production of any commodity or commodities required for domestic consumption; or (4) their equitable share, as determined by the Secretary, of the national production of any commodity or commodities required for domestic consumption and exports adjusted to reflect the extent to which their utilization of cropland on the farm conforms to farming practices which the Secretary determines will best effectuate the purposes specified in section 7 (a); or (5) any combination of the above. In arid or semiarid sections, (1) and (2) above shall be construed to cover water conservation and the beneficial use of water on individual farms, including measures to prevent run-off, the building of check dams and ponds, and providing facilities for applying water to the land. In determining the amount of any payment or grant measured by (1) or (2) the Secretary shall take into consideration the productivity of the land affected by the farming practices adopted during the year with respect to which such payment is made."

TITLE III—LOANS, PARITY PAYMENTS, CONSUMER SAFEGUARDS, AND MARKETING QUOTAS

SUBTITLE A—DEFINITIONS, LOANS, PARITY PAYMENTS, AND CONSUMER SAFEGUARDS

DEFINITIONS

SEC. 301. (a) GENERAL DEFINITIONS.—For the purposes of this title and the declaration of policy—

(1) "Parity," as applied to prices for any agricultural commodity, shall be that price for the commodity which will give to the commodity a purchasing power with respect to articles that farmers buy equivalent to the purchasing power of such commodity in the base period; and, in the case of all commodities for which the base period is the period August 1909 to July 1914, which will also reflect current interest payments per acre on farm indebtedness secured by real estate, tax payments per acre on farm real estate, and freight rates, as contrasted with such interest

payments, tax payments, and freight rates during the base period. The base period in the case of all agricultural commodities except tobacco shall be the period August 1909 to July 1914, and, in the case of tobacco, shall be the period August 1919 to July 1929.

(2) "Parity," as applied to income, shall be that per capita net income of individuals on farms from farming operations that bears to the per capita net income of individuals not on farms the same relation as prevailed during the period from August 1909 to July 1914. . . .

LOANS ON AGRICULTURAL COMMODITIES

SEC. 302. (a) The Commodity Credit Corporation is authorized, upon recommendation of the Secretary and with the approval of the President, to make available loans on agricultural commodities (including dairy products). Except as otherwise provided in this section, the amount, terms, and conditions of such loans shall be fixed by the Secretary, subject to the approval of the Corporation and the President.

(b) The Corporation is directed to make available to cooperators loans upon wheat during any marketing year beginning in a calendar year in which the farm price of wheat on June 15 is below 52 per centum of the parity price on such date, or the July crop estimate for wheat is in excess of a normal year's domestic consumption and exports, at rates not less than 52 per centum and not more than 75 per centum of the parity price of wheat at the beginning of the marketing year. In case marketing quotas for wheat are in effect in any marketing year, the Corporation is directed to make available, during such marketing year, to noncooperators, loans upon wheat at 60 per centum of the rate applicable to cooperators. A loan on wheat to a noncooperator shall be made only on so much of his wheat as would be subject to penalty if marketed.

(c) The Corporation is directed to make available to cooperators loans upon cotton during any marketing year beginning in a calendar year in which the average price on August 1 of seven-eighths Middling spot cotton on the ten markets designated by the Secretary is below 52 per centum of the parity price of cotton on such date, or the

August crop estimate for cotton is in excess of a normal year's domestic consumption and exports, at rates not less than 52 per centum and not more than 75 per centum of the parity price of cotton as of the beginning of the marketing year. In case marketing quotas for cotton are in effect in any marketing year, the Corporation is directed to make available, during such marketing year, to noncooperators, loans upon cotton at 60 per centum of the rate applicable to cooperators. A loan on cotton to a noncooperator shall be made only on so much of his cotton as would be subject to penalty if marketed.

(d) The Corporation is directed to make available loans upon corn during any marketing year beginning in the calendar year in which the November crop estimate for corn is in excess of a normal year's domestic consumption and exports, or in any marketing year when on November 15 the farm price of corn is below 75 per centum of the parity price, at the following rates:

> 75 per centum of such parity price if such estimate does not exceed a normal year's consumption and exports and the farm price of corn is below 75 per centum of the parity price on November 15;

> 70 per centum of such parity price if such estimate exceeds a normal year's domestic consumption and exports by not more than 10 per centum. . . .

PARITY PAYMENTS

SEC. 303. If and when appropriations are made therefor, the Secretary is authorized and directed to make payments to producers of corn, wheat, cotton, rice, or tobacco, on their normal production of such commodities in amounts which, together with the proceeds thereof, will provide a return to such producers which is as nearly equal to parity price as the funds so made available will permit. All funds available for such payments with respect to these commodities shall, unless otherwise provided by law, be apportioned to these commodities in proportion to the amount by which each fails to reach the parity income. Such payments shall be in addition to and not in substitution for any other payments authorized by law. . . .

PART III—MARKETING QUOTAS—WHEAT
LEGISLATIVE FINDINGS

SEC. 331. Wheat is a basic source of food for the Nation, is produced throughout the United States by more than a million farmers, is sold on the country-wide market and, as wheat or flour, flows almost entirely through instrumentalities of interstate and foreign commerce from producers to consumers.

Abnormally excessive and abnormally deficient supplies of wheat on the country-wide market acutely and directly affect, burden, and obstruct interstate and foreign commerce. Abnormally excessive supplies overtax the facilities of interstate and foreign transportation, congest terminal markets and milling centers in the flow of wheat from producers to consumers, depress the price of wheat in interstate and foreign commerce, and otherwise disrupt the orderly marketing of such commodity in such commerce. Abnormally deficient supplies result in an inadequate flow of wheat and its products in interstate and foreign commerce with consequent injurious effects to the instrumentalities of such commerce and with excessive increases in the prices of wheat and its products in interstate and foreign commerce.

It is in the interest of the general welfare that interstate and foreign commerce in wheat and its products be protected from such burdensome surpluses and distressing shortages, and that a supply of wheat be maintained which is adequate to meet domestic consumption and export requirements in years of drought, flood, and other adverse conditions as well as in years of plenty, and that the soil resources of the Nation be not wasted in the production of such burdensome surpluses. Such surpluses result in disastrously low prices of wheat and other grains to wheat producers, destroy the purchasing power of grain producers for industrial products, and reduce the value of the agricultural assets supporting the national credit structure. Such shortages of wheat result in unreasonably high prices of flour and bread to consumers and loss of market outlets by wheat producers.

The conditions affecting the production and marketing of wheat are such that, without Federal assistance, farmers, individually or in cooperation, cannot effectively prevent the recurrence of such surpluses and shortages and the burdens on interstate and foreign commerce resulting therefrom, maintain normal supplies of wheat, or provide for the orderly marketing thereof in interstate and foreign commerce.

The provisions of this Part affording a cooperative plan to wheat producers are necessary in order to minimize recurring surpluses and shortages of wheat in interstate and foreign commerce, to provide for the maintenance of adequate reserve supplies thereof, and to provide for an adequate flow of wheat and its products in interstate and foreign commerce. The provisions hereof for regulation of marketings by producers of wheat whenever an abnormally excessive supply of such commodity exists are necessary in order to maintain an orderly flow of wheat in interstate and foreign commerce under such conditions.

PROCLAMATIONS OF SUPPLIES AND ALLOTMENTS

SEC. 332. Not later than July 15 of each marketing year for wheat, the Secretary shall ascertain and proclaim the total supply and the normal supply of wheat for such marketing year, and the national acreage allotment for the next crop of wheat.

NATIONAL ACREAGE ALLOTMENT

SEC. 333. The national acreage allotment for any crop of wheat shall be that acreage which the Secretary determines will, on the basis of the national average yield for wheat, produce an amount thereof adequate, together with the estimated carry-over at the beginning of the marketing year for such crop, to make available a supply for such marketing year equal to a normal year's domestic consumption and exports plus 30 per centum thereof. The national acreage allotment for wheat for 1938 shall be sixty-two million five hundred thousand acres.

APPORTIONMENT OF NATIONAL ACREAGE ALLOTMENT

SEC. 334. (a) The national acreage allotment for wheat shall be apportioned by the Secretary among the several States on the basis of the acreage seeded for the production of wheat during the ten calendar years immediately preceding the calendar year in which the national acreage allotment is determined (plus, in applicable years, the acreage diverted under previous agricultural adjustment and conservation programs), with adjustments for abnormal weather conditions and for trends in acreage during such period.

MARKETING QUOTAS

SEC. 335. (a) Whenever it shall appear that the total supply of wheat as of the beginning of any marketing year will exceed a normal year's domestic consumption and exports by more than 35 per centum, the Secretary shall, not later than the May 15 prior to the beginning of such marketing year, proclaim such fact and, during the marketing year beginning July 1 and continuing throughout such marketing year, a national marketing quota shall be in effect with respect to the marketing of wheat. The Secretary shall ascertain and specify in the proclamation the amount of the national marketing quota in terms of a total quantity of wheat and also in terms of a marketing percentage of the national acreage allotment for the current crop which he determines will, on the basis of the national average yield of wheat, produce the amount of the national marketing quota. Marketing quotas for any marketing year shall be in effect with respect to wheat harvested in the calendar year in which such marketing year begins notwithstanding that the wheat is marketed prior to the beginning of such marketing year. No marketing quota with respect to the marketing of wheat shall be in effect for the marketing year beginning July 1, 1938, unless prior to the date of the proclamation of the Secretary, provision has been made by law for the payment, in whole or in part, in 1938 of parity payments with respect to wheat.

(b) The amount of the national marketing quota for wheat shall be equal to a normal year's domestic consumption and exports plus 30 per centum thereof, less the sum of (1) the estimated carry-over of wheat as of the beginning of the marketing year with respect to which the quota is proclaimed and (2) the estimated amount of wheat which will be used on farms as seed or livestock feed during the marketing year. . . .

THE EMPLOYMENT ACT OF FEBRUARY 20, 1946[21]

Concerned about recurrent recession in the American economy, plus the threat of inflation, Congress passed the Employment Act of 1946, undoubtedly a landmark in American legislative annals. Through the creation of a simple machinery—a Council of Economic Advisers in the President's Office and a Congressional Joint Committee on the Economic Report—it was hoped that the United States would be constantly alerted to dangers threatening the economy and that appropriate and immediate action could be taken as a result by the President, the Congress, and the Federal Reserve Board. There is no doubt that the brief postwar recessions of 1948-49, 1953-54, 1957-58, and 1960-61 had much of their sting removed because of the prompt measures taken under the Act.

✓   ✓   ✓

AN ACT

To declare a national policy on employment, production, and purchasing power, and for other purposes.

Be it enacted by the Senate and House of Representatives of the United States of America in Congress assembled,

SHORT TITLE

SECTION 1. This Act may be cited as the "Employment Act of 1946."

[21] *U. S. Statutes at Large,* Vol. 60, 79th Congress, 2nd Session, Ch. 33, pp. 23-25.

DECLARATION OF POLICY

SEC. 2. The Congress hereby declares that it is the continuing policy and responsibility of the Federal Government to use all practicable means consisting with its needs and obligations and other essential considerations of national policy, with the assistance and cooperation of industry, agriculture, labor, and State and local governments, to coordinate and utilize all its plans, functions, and resources for the purpose of creating and maintaining, in a manner calculated to foster and promote free competitive enterprise and the general welfare, conditions under which there will be afforded useful employment opportunities, including self-employment, for those able, willing, and seeking to work, and to promote maximum employment, production, and purchasing power.

ECONOMIC REPORT OF THE PRESIDENT

SEC. 3. (a) The President shall transmit to the Congress within sixty days after the beginning of each regular session (commencing with the year 1947) an economic report (hereinafter called the "Economic Report") setting forth (1) the levels of employment, production, and purchasing power obtaining in the United States and such levels needed to carry out the policy declared in section 2; (2) current and foreseeable trends in the levels of employment, production, and purchasing power; (3) a review of the economic program of the Federal Government and a review of economic conditions affecting employment in the United States or any considerable portion thereof during the preceding year and of their effect upon employment, production, and purchasing power; and (4) a program for carrying out the policy declared in section 2, together with such recommendations for legislation as he may deem necessary or desirable. . . .

COUNCIL OF ECONOMIC ADVISERS TO THE PRESIDENT

SEC. 4. (a) There is hereby created in the Executive Office of the President a Council of Economic Advisers (hereinafter called the "Council"). The Council shall be composed of three members who shall be appointed by the President, by and with the advice and consent of the

Senate, and each of whom shall be a person who, as a result of his training, experience, and attainments, is exceptionally qualified to analyze and interpret economic developments, to appraise programs and activities of the Government in the light of the policy declared in section 2, and to formulate and recommend national economic policy to promote employment, production, and purchasing power under free competitive enterprise. Each member of the Council shall receive compensation at the rate of $15,000 per annum. The President shall designate one of the members of the Council as chairman and one as vice chairman, who shall act as chairman in the absence of the chairman. . . .

(c) It shall be the duty and function of the Council—

(1) to assist and advise the President in the preparation of the Economic Report;

(2) to gather timely and authoritative information concerning economic developments and economic trends, both current and prospective, to analyze and interpret such information in the light of the policy declared in section 2 for the purpose of determining whether such developments and trends are interfering, or are likely to interfere, with the achievement of such policy, and to compile and submit to the President studies relating to such developments and trends;

(3) to appraise the various programs and activities of the Federal Government in the light of the policy declared in section 2 for the purpose of determining the extent to which such programs and activities are contributing, and the extent to which they are not contributing, to the achievement of such policy, and to make recommendations to the President with respect thereto;

(4) to develop and recommend to the President national economic policies to foster and promote free competitive enterprise, to avoid economic fluctuations or to diminish the effects thereof, and to maintain employment, production, and purchasing power;

(5) to make and furnish such studies, reports thereon, and recommendations with respect to matters of Federal economic policy and legislation as the President may request. . . .

JOINT COMMITTEE ON THE ECONOMIC REPORT

SEC. 5. (a) There is hereby established a Joint Committee on the Economic Report, to be composed of seven Members of the Senate, to be appointed by the President of the Senate, and seven Members of the House of Representatives, to be appointed by the Speaker of the House of Representatives. The party representation on the joint committee shall as nearly as may be feasible reflect the relative membership of the majority and minority parties in the Senate and House of Representatives.

(b) It shall be the function of the joint committee—

(1) to make a continuing study of matters relating to the Economic Report;

(2) to study means of coordinating programs in order to further the policy of this Act; and

(3) as a guide to the several committees of the Congress dealing with legislation relating to the Economic Report, not later than May 1 of each year (beginning with the year 1947) to file a report with the Senate and the House of Representatives containing its findings and recommendations with respect to each of the main recommendations made by the President in the Economic Report, and from time to time to make such other reports and recommendations to the Senate and House of Representatives as it deems advisable. . . .

— 22 —

THE TAFT-HARTLEY ACT OF JUNE 23, 1947[20]

The Wagner Act of 1935 had concerned itself with the unfair labor practices of management. The Taft-Hartley

[20] *U. S. Statutes at Large,* Vol. 61, 80th Congress, 1st Session, Ch. 120, pp. 141-159.

*Act of 1947 (known officially as the Labor-Management
Relations Act) turned to organized labor and forbade it
from engaging in specified unfair labor practices; too, it
gave the President of the United States the power to
declare a national emergency. When a strike threatened
to affect the welfare of the whole nation, during a period
of 80 days the strike had to cease while attempts at settlement were to be made by the Federal Mediation and Con-
ciliation Service. As regards restraints on unions, the Act
gave individuals the right to refuse to join unions under
certain circumstances and denied to unions the right to
insist upon the closed shop. Another interesting provision
required union officials of national or international unions
to file affidavits attesting that they were not members of
the Communist party. In 1959, Congress passed the Lan-
drum-Griffin Act which further restricted trade-union
activities, particularly as regards secondary boycotts; this
law also sought the Federal regulation of trade unions to
eliminate corruption and crime and to protect rank-and-
file union members in their rights as members of unions.*

✓   ✓   ✓

(b) It shall be an unfair labor practice for a labor organization or its agents—

(1) to restrain or coerce (A) employees in the exercise of the rights guaranteed in section 7: *Provided,*
That this paragraph shall not impair the right of a labor
organization to prescribe its own rules with respect to
the acquisition or retention of membership therein; or
(B) an employer in the selection of his representatives
for the purposes of collective bargaining or the adjustment of grievances;

(2) to cause or attempt to cause an employer to discriminate against an employee in violation of subsection
(a) (3) or to discriminate against an employee with
respect to whom membership in such organization has
been denied or terminated on some ground other than
his failure to tender the periodic dues and the initiation
fees uniformly required as a condition of acquiring or
retaining membership;

(3) to refuse to bargain collectively with an em-

ployer, provided it is the representative of his employees subject to the provisions of section 9 (a) ;

(4) to engage in, or to induce or encourage the employees of any employer to engage in, a strike or a concerted refusal in the course of their employment to use, manufacture, process, transport, or otherwise handle or work on any goods, articles, materials, or commodities or to perform any services, where an object thereof is : (A) forcing or requiring any employer or self-employed person to join any labor or employer organization or any employer or other person to cease using, selling, handling, transporting, or otherwise dealing in the products of any other producer, processor, or manufacturer, or to cease doing business with any other person; (B) forcing or requiring any other employer to recognize or bargain with a labor organization as the representative of his employees unless such labor organization has been certified as the representative of such employees under the provisions of section 9; (C) forcing or requiring any employer to recognize or bargain with a particular labor organization as the representative of his employees if another labor organization has been certified as the representative of such employees under the provisions of section 9; (D) forcing or requiring any employer to assign particular work to employees in a particular labor organization or in a particular trade, craft, or class rather than to employees in another labor organization or in another trade, craft, or class, unless such employer is failing to conform to an order or certification of the Board determining the bargaining representative for employees performing such work: *Provided,* That nothing contained in this subsection (b) shall be construed to make unlawful a refusal by any person to enter upon the premises of any employer (other than his own employer), if the employees of such employer are engaged in a strike ratified or approved by a representative of such employees whom such employer is required to recognize under this Act;

(5) to require of employees covered by an agreement authorized under subsection (a) (3) the payment, as a condition precedent to becoming a member of such

organization, of a fee in an amount which the Board finds excessive or discriminatory under all the circumstances. In making such a finding, the Board shall consider, among other relevant factors, the practices and customs of labor organizations in the particular industry, and the wages currently paid to the employees affected; and

(6) to cause or attempt to cause an employer to pay or deliver or agree to pay or deliver any money or other thing of value, in the nature of an exaction, for services which are not performed or not to be performed.

(c) The expressing of any views, argument, or opinion, or the dissemination thereof, whether in written, printed, graphic, or visual form, shall not constitute or be evidence of an unfair labor practice under any of the provisions of this Act, if such expression contains no threat of reprisal or force or promise of benefit. . . .

NATIONAL EMERGENCIES

SEC. 206. Whenever in the opinion of the President of the United States, a threatened or actual strike or lock-out affecting an entire industry or a substantial part thereof engaged in trade, commerce, transportation, transmission, or communication among the several States or with foreign nations, or engaged in the production of goods for commerce, will, if permitted to occur or to continue, imperil the national health or safety, he may appoint a board of inquiry to inquire into the issues involved in the dispute and to make a written report to him within such time as he shall prescribe. Such report shall include a statement of the facts with respect to the dispute, including each party's statement of its position but shall not contain any recommendations. The President shall file a copy of such report with the Service and shall make its contents available to the public. . . .

SEC. 208. (a) Upon receiving a report from a board of inquiry the President may direct the Attorney General to petition any district court of the United States having jurisdiction of the parties to enjoin such strike or lock-out or the continuing thereof, and if the court finds that such threatened or actual strike or lock-out—

(i) affects an entire industry or a substantial

part thereof engaged in trade, commerce, transportation, transmission, or communication among the several States or with foreign nations, or engaged in the production of goods for commerce; and

(ii) if permitted to occur or to continue, will imperil the national health or safety, it shall have jurisdiction to enjoin any such strike or lock-out, or the continuing thereof, and to make such other orders as may be appropriate. . . .

(b) Upon the issuance of such order, the President shall reconvene the board of inquiry which has previously reported with respect to the dispute. At the end of a sixty-day period (unless the dispute has been settled by that time), the board of inquiry shall report to the President the current position of the parties and the efforts which have been made for settlement, and shall include a statement by each party of its position and a statement of the employer's last offer of settlement. The President shall make such report available to the public. The National Labor Relations Board, within the succeeding fifteen days, shall take a secret ballot of the employees of each employer involved in the dispute on the question of whether they wish to accept the final offer of settlement made by their employer as stated by him and shall certify the results thereof to the Attorney General within five days thereafter.

SEC. 210. Upon the certification of the results of such ballot or upon a settlement being reached, whichever happens sooner, the Attorney General shall move the court to discharge the injunction, which motion shall then be granted and the injunction discharged. When such motion is granted, the President shall submit to the Congress a full and comprehensive report of the proceedings, including the findings of the board of inquiry and the ballot taken by the National Labor Relations Board, together with such recommendations as he may see fit to make for consideration and appropriate action. . . .

BOYCOTTS AND OTHER UNLAWFUL COMBINATIONS

SEC. 303. (a) It shall be unlawful, for the purposes of this section only, in an industry or activity affecting commerce, for any labor organization to engage in, or to induce or encourage the employees of any employer to engage in, a strike or a concerted refusal in the course of their employment to use, manufacture, process, transport, or otherwise handle or work on any goods, articles, materials, or commodities or to perform any services, where an object thereof is—

(1) forcing or requiring any employer or self-employed person to join any labor or employer organization or any employer or other person to cease using, selling, handling, transporting, or otherwise dealing in the products of any other producer, processor, or manufacturer, or to cease doing business with any other person;

(2) forcing or requiring any other employer to recognize or bargain with a labor organization as the representative of his employees unless such labor organization has been certified as the representative of such employees under the provisions of section 9 of the National Labor Relations Act;

(3) forcing or requiring any employer to recognize or bargain with a particular labor organization as the representative of his employees if another labor organization has been certified as the representative of such employees under the provisions of section 9 of the National Labor Relations Act;

(4) forcing or requiring any employer to assign particular work to employees in a particular labor organization or in a particular trade, craft, or class rather than to employees in another labor organization or in another trade, craft, or class unless such employer is failing to conform to an order or certification of the National Labor Relations Board determining the bargaining representative for employees performing such work. Nothing contained in this subsection shall be construed to make unlawful a refusal by any person to enter upon the premises of any employer (other than his own employer), if the employees of such employer are engaged in a strike ratified or approved by a representative of such employees whom such employer is required to recognize under the National Labor Relations Act.

(b) Whoever shall be injured in his business or property by reason or any violation of subsection (a) may sue therefor in any district court of the United States subject to the limitations and provisions of section 301 hereof without respect to the amount in controversy, or in any other court having jurisdiction of the parties, and shall recover the damages by him sustained and the cost of the suit.

RESTRICTION ON POLITICAL CONTRIBUTIONS

SEC. 304. Section 313 of the Federal Corrupt Practices Act, 1925 (U. S. C., 1940 edition, title 2, sec. 251; Supp. V, title 50, App., sec. 1509), as amended, is amended to read as follows:

SEC. 313. It is unlawful for any national bank, or any corporation organized by authority of any law of Congress, to make a contribution or expenditure in connection with any election to any political office, or in connection with any primary election or political convention or caucus held to select candidates for any political office, or for any corporation whatever, or any labor organization to make a contribution or expenditure in connection with any election at which Presidential and Vice Presidential electors or a Senator or Representative in, or a Delegate or Resident Commissioner to Congress are to be voted for, or in connection with any primary election or political convention or caucus held to select candidates for any of the foregoing offices, or for any candidate, political committee, or other person to accept or receive any contribution prohibited by this section. . . .

23

UNITED STATES PRIVATE FOREIGN INVESTMENTS, 1957[23]

Up to 1915, the United States had continued to be a debtor nation, borrowing more from foreigners than we lent to them. From 1915 on, American investments abroad mounted and in the year 1957 private investments alone came to nearly $4 billion. The total for direct foreign investments was $25.3 billion, with annual earnings of $3.3 billion. These figures did not include private long-term portfolio investments, loans extended to foreigners, and United States government credits and loans. As of 1959, total American investments abroad (including all the above categories) came to $64.8 billion. Foreign investments in the U. S. on the other hand came to $40.7 billion; the balance in our favor therefore was $24.1 billion.

✓   ✓   ✓

In 1957, for the second successive year, private United States foreign investments were nearly $4 billion. Direct investments by United States companies in their foreign branches and subsidiaries increased more than $3 billion reaching a total book value of over $25 billion by the end of 1957.

Part of the expansion in direct investments in both 1956 and 1957 was attributable to large cash payments for newly acquired properties or oil leases, but most of the stepped-up outflow reflected continued expectations of strong long-run demand for basic materials here and abroad, coupled with a tendency to establish production facilities abroad to supply foreign markets.

Other private capital investment in 1957 totaled $1.1

[23] United States Department of Commerce, *Survey of Current Business* (September, 1958), pp. 15-22.

118

billion, mainly representing purchases of foreign dollar bonds and long- and short-term bank loans. . . .

Earnings on private foreign investments advanced to a high of $3.7 billion in 1957, nearly $300 million more than the 1956 amount, reflecting the rapidly growing amount of capital invested. Over two-thirds of the gain was accounted for by direct investments, even though much of the investment outlay in the past 2 years has been in properties which are not yet fully productive. Interest and dividend receipts from portfolio and short-term investments rose considerably as these investments expanded.

The geographic distribution of direct investment in 1957 showed as usual a concentration in the Western Hemisphere and Europe, which accounted for seven-eighths of the total . . . investments in less developed countries since 1950 have been largely in petroleum and mining, with the notable exception of some Latin American countries where both local and foreign capital are now developing the industrial and market potential.

Resource development with the aid of foreign capital is often the most effective initial stimulus to rising national incomes, especially since it is usually accompanied by the construction of transportation and other public utilities. In this connection, it is significant that a number of investment projects just beginning or under consideration involve large outlays for resource development in areas where private United States investment has previously not been large. . . .

Despite recurring crises, the flow of United States direct investment capital to the Middle East area held at an annual rate of about $100 million in 1956 and 1957. There were sharp fluctuations in the flow of funds to individual parts of the area, but these often reflected temporary variations in cash positions rather than trends in fixed investment or exploration and development. The latter activity is going forward extensively, and in addition to the sums accounted for as capital expenditures, roughly $25 million was spent in essentially non-producing countries in the Middle East and North Africa in the search for additional reserves.

The current rate of capital outflow to this area is less than in earlier postwar years, when production was being rapidly expanded. Crude oil produced in the Middle East by United States operators, or as their share of joint operations, fluctuated widely as a result of the Suez crisis and later developments, but averaged 2 million barrels per day in 1957, about 50 per cent of the total produced in the free world outside the Western Hemisphere. Major expenditures are in prospect for the area to develop new reserves in North Africa, in offshore locations, and in Iran, and in unproven areas.

BOOK VALUES, $25.3 BILLION

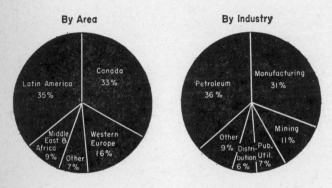

EARNINGS, $3.3 BILLION

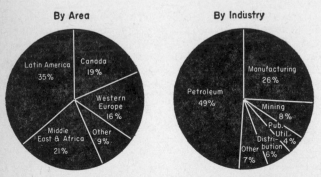

DISTRIBUTION OF UNITED STATES
DIRECT FOREIGN INVESTMENT, 1957

Investments in Africa south of the Sahara increased by about $40 million in 1957, exclusive of shipping companies in Liberia. This was less than the 1956 rate, as there were sharp reductions in the outflow of capital for petroleum investment, especially for the Union of South Africa.

In the past year there has been a notable rise in interest by United States business concerns in the possible development of the mineral resources of parts of the African continent in which United States investment has been small or nonexistent. Some of the contemplated investments are comparatively large and could be significant steps in the economic development of this area.

A steady rate of investment was maintained in the Far East, yielding an increase in direct investments of about $175 million for 1957. Additions to investments in Australia were about $50 million, mainly for manufacturing plants. The rise in Indonesia largely reflected petroleum activities, and in Japan the principal industry showing increases was manufacturing, with petroleum also higher than in 1956. Increases in the Philippine Republic were spread over several industries. Elsewhere in the Far East there was little growth of United States direct investments in 1957, and the total invested to the end of 1957, outside of the countries mentioned above, was comparatively small.

On an industry basis, investments in the petroleum industry dominated the growth of direct investments in 1957, increasing by $1.7 billion to a total book value of about $9 billion. Over half of the rise was in Latin America, with Venezuela far in the lead. Output by United States companies in Venezuela reached a high of a little over 2 million barrels per day during the Suez crisis, when Middle East production was cut back, and averaged 1.9 million barrels per day in 1957, up about 9 per cent over 1956 output.

Most of the Latin American increase was financed by larger capital outflows from the United States, and reinvested earnings were also higher. Parent companies in the United States were under considerable pressure to raise the funds required for expansion in this and other areas, and placed several large security issues in the United States capital market.

Petroleum investments in Canada were again large in

1957, and in Europe also the flow was maintained in substantial amounts, particularly to the United Kingdom and Germany. In the Middle East and North Africa, petroleum accounted for practically all United States investment, with the outflow of somewhat over $100 million about the same as in 1956. The rate of investment was considerably cut back elsewhere in Africa, and was also off in the Far East.

Manufacturing currently ranks next to petroleum as a field for United States direct foreign investments, with additional investments of over $750 million in 1957 raising the total value of such investments to $7.9 billion. Investment in this industry was slightly less than in 1956 because of smaller reinvestments of earnings. The outflow of capital, on the other hand, rose substantially.

Canada has received about 40 per cent of United States direct manufacturing investments abroad in the past 2 years. Although manufacturing earnings in Canada were down sharply in 1957, additional capital supplied by parent companies was sufficient to offset most of the decline in investment funds available out of earnings.

In Western Europe, additions to manufacturing investments were maintained at an annual rate of over $200 million. Investment in manufacturing in the United Kingdom predominates, with Germany and Italy receiving sizable, though lesser, amounts. In the rest of the world, manufacturing investments continued to rise significantly in Australia, the Union of South Africa, and Japan.

Among other industries, mining and smelting investments showed a sizable increase in 1957, despite a sharp decline in earnings resulting from lower prices for metals and minerals. Capital moving to Latin America for mining investments rose steeply, with substantial amounts going to Chile, Peru, and Mexico. A number of large new projects are in prospect for South America and the Caribbean area. Mining investments in Canada were substantial in 1957, though reinvested earnings were smaller. Sizable new projects are also underway in that country.

Public utility investments rose somewhat in 1957, although remaining comparatively low. Most of the investment went to Latin America, largely to Cuba, Venezuela, and Brazil. Panamanian shipping companies reinvested substantial amounts and received additional sums from parent companies. . . .

It is particularly difficult to trace the investments of the shipping subsidiaries, and sizable amounts shown for Panama or Liberia may actually be utilized elsewhere to meet the requirements of the parent companies. The growing number of holding company arrangements also increases the difficulty of determining the countries in which actual investments are occurring.

Direct investments in agricultural enterprises resulted in a net reduction on balance because of the sale of sizable properties. Investments in trade, finance, and service establishments abroad form a sizable portion of all direct investments, having an aggregate book value of $3.2 billion at the end of 1957. The increase of $300 million in 1957 was less than in 1956, largely because of reduced capital outflows to finance organizations in Canada. There were also reductions in these investments in several Latin-American countries.

Private United States capital for long-term portfolio investments abroad amounted to more than $800 million in 1957, and about $300 million of short-term private credits were extended to foreign borrowers. The combined total of $1.1 billion was about equal to the 1956 amount, but the proportion of short-term capital was lower in 1957.

New issues of foreign dollar bonds sold in the United States totaled about $600 million in 1957. . . . Nearly $200 million was also raised by the International Bank for Reconstruction and Development, and small amounts were obtained by a growing list of other borrowers. . . .

Net purchases by United States investors of outstanding foreign corporate stocks amounted to only $33 million in 1957, compared with over $100 million in 1956. Purchases of such securities, principally issues of Canadian and large European corporations, had been substantial from 1953 to the time of the Suez crisis in 1956. Thereafter, purchases of the Canadian issues continued in considerable volume, but there was a net liquidation of European stocks through 1957. In the first half of 1958, purchases of European stocks were resumed, reflecting generally prosperous conditions in these countries. Net purchases of outstanding foreign bonds continued in 1957 and 1958 on a modest scale.

Loans extended to foreigners, both short-term and those with maturities of up to about 5 years, increased by a net amount of nearly $600 million in 1957 . . . the total of these claims and loans outstanding at the end of 1957 was $4.1 billion. Principal recipients of this financing in 1957 were France, the United Kingdom (partly to finance purchases of oil leases), Brazil, Mexico, Venezuela, and a few Asian countries.

The availability of bank financing has been important for these countries, and has helped to reduce the severity of fluctuations in United States and world trade. . . .

Long-term United States Government credits and loans to foreign countries outstanding at the end of 1957 were about $330 million higher than a year earlier, with gross disbursements during the year of nearly $1 billion the highest since 1948, while repayments of about $660 million were a record high. Over 40 per cent of the net outflow, or about $145 million, was to Latin America, mainly as Export-Import Bank loans. The net outflow to Western Europe was about the same, although both disbursements and repayments were larger than for Latin America. The outflow to Europe included a $250 million drawing against the $500 million Export-Import Bank loan to the United Kingdom, which was provided at the time of the Suez crisis to support sterling area reserves. For most other European countries repayments exceeded new loans. Although the net outflow to the rest of the world was small, this was the result of large repayments by India and Pakistan of silver loaned under lend-lease arrangements, while disbursements were as large as in the previous year.

Beginning in 1954, the fastest growing component of United States Government foreign assets has been the accumulation of foreign currencies, or equivalent claims, derived from the sale of surplus agricultural commodities. In 1957, the net short-term capital outflow associated with these assets was $635 million . . .

Earnings of direct private foreign investments, which account for about seven-eighths of total earnings on foreign investments, increased by nearly 7 per cent in 1957 to over $3.3 billion. Virtually the whole increased flowed from the petroleum industry, reflecting generally maintained production—although declines in the Middle East early in the year were offset by increased output in Latin America—and a strong demand situation. Petroleum earnings in 1957 accounted for nearly half of the direct investment total. . . .

Most other industries did not fare so well. Agriculture, public utilities, and trade, finance and service enterprises reported marginal gains over the 1956 results. In agriculture, profits of sugar properties were better with the improved sugar market, but other branches of the industry earned about the same amount as in 1956.

Earnings of mining and smelting enterprises fell by nearly 20 per cent in 1957, as metal and mineral prices reacted from earlier highs. . . .

Aggregate earnings of United States-owned manufacturing plants abroad were about $850 million in 1957, only slightly lower than in 1956. . . .

The reinvestment of foreign earnings of United States corporations, amounting to about $1 billion annually in 1956 and 1957, continued to be a major source of financing for expanding their foreign enterprises. Over half of the earnings of foreign subsidiary companies remained undistributed in 1957. . . .

Dividends and interest received from private portfolio and short-term investments abroad rose substantially in 1957 to a total of over $360 million. About one-third of this income is earned on United States holdings of foreign dollar bonds, which have been expanding steadily and generally under conditions of rising yields. Rapidly growing long- and short-term banks loans outstanding, at rising interest rates, have also resulted in larger interest receipts.

24

THE HIGHWAY ACT OF AUGUST 27, 1958[24]

In 1956, Congress sat down to rewrite the Federal law that had been devised to aid in the construction of roads in 1916; and it revised and codified the whole system in 1958. In all, 41,000 miles of road were to be constructed by 1972 and up to $25 billion was to be expended on a 90-10 matching basis with the States. By 1960, experts were estimating that the cost was likely to be $37 billion rather than $25 billion. Nothing exemplified more the expanding functions of the Federal government into areas hitherto regarded as entirely or largely State concerns. Professor William G. Carleton, writing in "Political Science Quarterly," has pointed out that Federal grants-in-aid have increased from $3 million in 1901 to $615 million in 1941 and to $7 billion currently (counting the so-called highway trust fund).

✓   ✓   ✓

CH. I. FEDERAL-AID HIGHWAYS

SEC. 101. *Declaration of policy.*—(b) It is hereby declared to be in the national interest to accelerate the construction of the Federal-aid highway systems, including the National System of Interstate and Defense Highways, since many of such highways, or portions thereof, are in fact inadequate to meet the needs of local and interstate commerce, for the national and civil defense.

It is hereby declared that the prompt and early completion of the National System of Interstate and Defense

[24] United States Department of Commerce, Bureau of Public Roads. *Federal Laws. . . . Relating to Highways* (1960), pp. 1-45.

Highways, so named because of its primary importance to the national defense and hereafter referred to as the "Interstate System," is essential to the national interest and is one of the most important objectives of this Act. It is the intent of Congress that the Interstate System be completed as nearly as practicable over the period of availability of the thirteen years' appropriations authorized for the purpose of expediting its construction, reconstruction, or improvement, inclusive of necessary tunnels and bridges, through the fiscal year ending June 30, 1969, under section 108(b) of the Federal-Aid Highway Act of 1956 (70 Stat. 374), and that the entire System in all States be brought to simultaneous completion. Insofar as possible in consonance with this objective, existing highways located on an interstate route shall be used to the extent that such use is practicable, suitable, and feasible, it being the intent that local needs, to the extent practicable, suitable, and feasible, shall be given equal consideration with the needs of interstate commerce. . . .

SEC. 103. *Federal-aid systems.*—(a) For the purposes of this title, the three Federal-aid systems, the primary and secondary systems, and the Interstate System, are continued pursuant to the provisions of this section.

(b) The Federal-aid primary system shall consist of an adequate system of connected main highways, selected or designated by each State through its State highway department, subject to the approval of the Secretary as provided by subsection (e) of this section. This system shall not exceed 7 per centum of the total highway mileage of such State, exclusive of mileage within national forests, Indian, or other Federal reservations and within urban areas, as shown by the records of the State highway department on November 9, 1921. Whenever provision has been made by any State for the completion and maintenance of 90 per centum of its Federal-aid primary system, as originally designated, said State through its State highway department by and with the approval of the Secretary is authorized to increase the mileage of its Federal-aid primary system by additional mileage equal to not more than 1 per centum of the total mileage of said State as shown by the records on November 9, 1921. Thereafter, it may make like 1 per centum increases in the mileage of its Federal-aid primary system whenever provision has been made for the completion and maintenance of 90 per centum of the entire system, including the additional mileage previously authorized. This system may be located both in rural and urban areas. The mileage limitations in this paragraph shall not apply to the District of Columbia, Hawaii, Alaska, or Puerto Rico.

(c) The Federal-aid secondary system shall be selected by the State highway departments and the appropriate local road officials in cooperation with each other, subject to approval by the Secretary as provided in subsection (e) of this section. In making such selections, farm-to-market roads, rural mail routes, public school bus routes, local rural roads, county roads, township roads, and roads of the county road class may be included, so long as they are not on the Federal-aid primary system or the Interstate System. This system shall be confined to rural areas, except (1) that in any State having a population density of more than two hundred per square mile as shown by the latest available Federal census, the system may include mileage in urban areas as well as rural, and (2) that the system may be extended into urban areas subject to the conditions that any such extension passes through the urban area or connects with another Federal-aid system within the urban area, and that Federal participation in projects on such extensions is limited to urban funds.

(d) The Interstate System shall be designated within the United States, including the District of Columbia, and it shall not exceed forty-one thousand miles in total extent. It shall be so located as to connect by routes, as direct as practicable, the principal metropolitan areas, cities, and industrial centers, to serve the national defense and, to the greatest extent possible, to connect at suitable border points with routes of continental importance in the Dominion of Canada and the Republic of Mexico. The routes of this system, to the greatest extent possible, shall be selected by joint action of the State highway departments of each State and the adjoining States, subject to the approval by the Secretary as provided in subsection (e) of this section. All highways or routes included in the Interstate System are finally approved, if not already coincident with the primary system, shall be added to said system without regard to the mileage limitation set forth in subsection (b) of this section. This system may be located both in rural and urban areas. . . .

SEC. 105. *Programs.*—(a) As soon as practicable after the apportionments for the Federal-aid systems have been made for any fiscal year, the State highway department of any State desiring to avail itself of the benefits of this chapter shall submit to the Secretary for his approval a program or programs of proposed projects for the utilization of the funds apportioned. The Secretary shall act upon programs submitted to him as soon as practicable after the same have been submitted. The Secretary may approve a program in whole or in part, but he shall not approve any project in a proposed program which is not located upon an approved Federal-aid system.

(b) In approving programs for projects on the Federal-aid secondary system, the Secretary shall require, except in States where all public roads and highways are under the control and supervision of the State highway department, that such project be selected by the State highway department and the appropriate local officials in cooperation with each other.

(c) In approving programs for projects on the Federal-aid primary system, the Secretary shall give preference to such projects as will expedite the completion of an adequate and connected system of highways interstate in character.

(d) In approving programs for projects under this chapter, the Secretary may give priority of approval to, and expedite the construction of, projects that are recommended as important to the national defense by the Secretary of Defense, or other official authorized by the President to make such recommendation. . . .

SEC. 109. *Standards.*—(a) The Secretary shall not approve plans and specifications for proposed projects on any Federal-aid system if they fail to provide for a facility (1) that will adequately meet the existing and probable future traffic needs and conditions in a manner conducive to safety, durability, and economy of maintenance; (2) that will be designed and constructed in accordance with standards best suited to accomplish the foregoing objectives and to conform to the particular needs of each locality.

(b) The geometric and construction standards to be adopted for the Interstate System shall be those approved by the Secretary in cooperation with the State highway departments. Such standards shall be adequate to accommodate the types and volumes of traffic forecast for the year 1975. The right-of-way width of the Interstate System shall be adequate to permit construction of projects on the Interstate System up to such standards. The Secretary shall apply such standards uniformly throughout the States.

(c) Projects on the Federal-aid secondary system in which Federal funds participate shall be constructed according to specifications that will provide all-weather service and permit maintenance at a reasonable cost. . . .

(e) No funds shall be approved for expenditure on any Federal-aid highway, or highway affected under chapter 2 of this title, unless proper safety protective devices complying with safety standards determined by the Secretary at that time as being adequate shall be installed or be in operation at any highway and railroad grade crossing or drawbridge on that portion of the highway with respect to which such expenditures are to be made. . . .

SEC. 111. *Agreements relating to use of and access to rights-of-way—Interstate System.*—All agreements between the Secretary and the State highway department for the construction of projects on the Interstate System shall contain a clause providing that the State will not add any points of access to, or exit from, the project in addition to those approved by the Secretary in the plans for such project, without the prior approval of the Secretary. Such agreements shall also contain a clause providing that the State will not permit automotive service stations or other commercial establishments for serving motor vehicle users to be constructed or located on the rights-of-way of the Interstate System. Such agreements may, however, authorize a State or political subdivision thereof to use the airspace above and below the established grade line of the highway payment for the parking of motor vehicles provided such use does not interfere in any way with the free flow of traffic on the Interstate System.

Sec. 112. *Letting of contracts.*—(a) In all cases where the construction is to be performed by the State highway department or under its supervision, a request for submission of bids shall be made by advertisement unless some other method is approved by the Secretary. The Secretary shall require such plans and specifications and such methods of bidding as shall be effective in securing competition.

(b) Construction of each project, subject to the provisions of subsection (a) of this section, shall be performed by contract awarded by competitive bidding, unless the Secretary shall affirmatively find that, under the circumstances relating to such project, some other method is in the public interest. All such findings shall be reported promptly in writing to the Committees on Public Works of the Senate and the House of Representatives. . . .

Sec. 120. *Federal share payable.*—(a) Subject to the provisions of subsection (d) of this section, the Federal share payable on account of any project, financed with primary, secondary, or urban funds, on the Federal-aid primary system and the Federal-aid secondary system shall not exceed 50 per centum of the cost of construction, except that in the case of any State containing nontaxable Indian lands, individual and tribal, and public domain lands (both reserved and unreserved) exclusive of national forests and national parks and monuments, exceeding 5 per centum of the total area of all lands therein, the Federal share shall be increased by a percentage of the remaining cost equal to the percentage that the area of all such lands in such State, is of its total area.

(b) Subject to the provisions of subsection (d) of this section, the Federal share payable on account of any project, financed with interstate funds on the Interstate System, authorized to be appropriated prior to June 29, 1956, shall not exceed 60 per centum of the cost of construction, except that in the case of any State containing unappropriated and unreserved public lands and nontaxable Indian lands, individual and tribal, exceeding 5 per centum of the total area of all lands therein, the Federal share shall be increased by a percentage of the remaining cost equal to the percentage that the area of all such lands in such State, is of its total area. The provisions of subsection (a) of this section shall apply to any project financed with funds authorized by the provisions of section 2 of the Federal-Aid Highway Act of 1952.

(c) Subject to the provisions of subsection (d) of this section, the Federal share payable on account of any project on the Interstate System provided for by funds made available under the provisions of section 108(b) of the Federal-Aid Highway Act of 1956 shall be increased to 90 per centum of the total cost thereof, plus a percentage of the remaining 10 per centum of such cost in any State containing unappropriated and unreserved public lands and nontaxable Indian lands, individual and tribal, exceeding 5 per centum of the total area of all lands therein, equal to the percentage that the area of such lands in such State is of its total area, except that such Federal share payable on any project in any State shall not exceed 95 per centum of the total cost of such project.

(d) The Federal share payable on account of any project for the elimination of hazards of railway-highway crossings, as more fully described and subject to the conditions and limitations set forth in section 130 of this title, may amount to 100 per centum of the cost of construction of such projects, except that not more than 50 per centum of the right-of-way and property damage costs, paid from public funds, on any such project, may be paid from sums apportioned in accordance with section 104 of this title: *Provided,* That not more than 10 per centum of all the sums apportioned for all the Federal-aid systems for any fiscal year in accordance with section 104 of this title shall be used under this subsection. . . .

SEC. 121. *Payment to States for construction.*—(a) The Secretary may, in his discretion, from time to time as the work progresses, make payments to a State for costs of construction incurred by it on a project. These payments shall at no time exceed the Federal share of the costs of construction incurred to the date of the voucher covering such payment plus the Federal share of the value of the materials which have been stockpiled in the vicinity of such construction in conformity to plans and specifications for the project.

(b) After completion of a project in accordance with the plans and specifications, and approval of the final voucher by the Secretary, a State shall be entitled to payment out of the appropriate sums apportioned to it of the unpaid balance of the Federal share payable on account of such project.

(c) No payment shall be made under this chapter, except for a project located on a Federal-aid system and covered by a project agreement. No final payment shall be made to a State for its costs of construction of a project until the completion of the construction has been approved by the Secretary following inspections pursuant to section 114(a) of this title.

— 25 —

ECONOMIC GROWTH AND PROGRESS, THE 1950'S [25]

Beginning with 1932, at the request of the Senate, the Department of Commerce began to study the National Income of the United States, its analyses and computations being enormously assisted by the pioneer work of Simon Kuznets of the National Bureau of Economic Research. More and more, the accent shifted over from income to product analysis and by 1947 the Department of Commerce was ready to offer in statistical terms, as it has said, "a comprehensive national economic accounting system designed to provide an integrated over-all view of the economic structure and process." This is being done through an analysis of the Gross National Product, or Expendi-

[25] United States Department of Commerce, Office of Business Statistics, *U. S. Income and Output. The Economy Viewed through the National Income Accounts* (Washington, 1958), pp. 1-25.

tures, of the United States in constant dollars. Gross National Product, as the Department of Commerce defines it, is the market value of the output of goods and services produced by the nation's economy, before deduction of depreciation charges and other allowances for business and institutional consumption of durable capital goods. Gross National Product therefore includes the purchase of goods and services by consumers and government, gross private domestic investment (including the change in business inventories), and net foreign investment.

The statement that follows is a typical one issued periodically by the Department of Commerce. It reports the experiences of the economy from the end of the war to midsummer 1958. Its tone of confidence is to be noted; the general feeling was that the country was having no problems overcoming short-lived recessions.

✓   ✓   ✓

GENERAL CONSIDERATIONS

Growth and progress have constituted the outstanding feature of the American economy in the postwar period. The physical volume of total output in 1957 was more than two-fifths above that of 10 years earlier; on a per capita basis, output was up more than one-fifth.

The postwar economic expansion has been a continuation of the longer-term course of developments in this country. . . .

While growth in the past decade has not been a steady process, the postwar setbacks to business have been mild. With a concatenation of forceful influences—some temporary and some of a longer-term character—conducive to expansion, prosperous conditions have prevailed throughout most of the past decade. The standard of living has improved substantially.

Postwar developments have reflected primarily continued operation of the same basic forces that have characterized our economic life in the past. However, new factors have also been at work. Government has played an increasing role, in the main to meet the defense requirements of the cold war but also to discharge added responsibilities in the civilian sphere through a broad range of social and economic programs.

Another set of factors influencing the postwar scene was the abnormality of demand and supply conditions immediately after the war. On the one hand, there was a translation into effective demand of consumption and investment that had been postponed during World War II and the 1930's. On the other, capacity to produce civilian goods was limited pending the completion of economic reconversion. Because of these circumstances, the rate of economic advance was above average in the first half of the decade.

In these years, technological progress that had been latent during the depression and unusually rapid under the exigencies of war, became embodied in civilian production on a large scale. However, continuous improvements in the techniques and organization of production were an outstanding feature of the entire postwar period, and were both a cause and an effect of the generally high rate of business investment.

It seems appropriate at this point to review our progress —to establish its dimensions and characteristics, and to assay our current status not only in the light of the more recent past but in broader historical perspective. . . .

EXPANSION OF THE POSTWAR ECONOMY

Gross national product in 1957 was valued at $440 billion, as compared with $234 billion 10 years earlier. Over this period, prices rose 30 per cent. Much of the advance reflected the aftermath of World War II, and another spurt came with the Korean conflict, but pressures on the price level were characteristic of the entire period. After adjustment for the price factor, aggregate output expanded, as already indicated, by more than two-fifths over the decade. . . .

The decade started from a relatively low base. Investment had lagged in the 1930's; and during the war the stock of capital available for peacetime use had been depleted by heavy wear-and-tear and by the need to channel resources into the production of facilities and munitions required directly for the war effort. Moreover, employment and real output immediately after the war were affected by the technical and organizational bottlenecks associated with the transition to peacetime production.

Productive capacity was thus capable of very rapid expansion from the early postwar base. Demand factors were also conducive to a swift rise of output. Consumers had had to defer demand on a large scale during the war, and correspondingly had accumulated financial resources which greatly improved their liquidity positions. Backlog demands made themselves felt extensively in consumer markets once wartime restrictions had been removed.

Another factor affecting the consumer market was rapid population growth. Population had not sustained its earlier expansion during the 1930's, when the increase was roughly half that of the preceding decade. The birthrate began to rise during the war and this rise was further accentuated after the termination of hostilities. Similarly, the rate of new family formation was particularly high during the early postwar period. These demographic developments reinforced the buoyancy of consumer demand.

Incentives to invest were also powerful. Against the background of a receptive consumer market, the business community was eager to make up for capital depletion in the prior span of years, to incorporate in productive facilities past advances in technology, and to lay the basis for further expansion on a broad scale. As in the case of consumers, liquid resources accumulated during the war helped to finance postwar expenditures. After-tax profits, which had been restrained during the war, assumed a more normal relationship to sales as taxes were lowered and other wartime controls removed.

Foreign markets also had an influence on United States production that was special to this period. Some of our customers abroad were in a backlog-demand and liquid-asset position analogous to that of domestic buyer groups. Other foreign countries, whose productive operations had been seriously damaged and disorganized by the war, needed to supplement their current output, both in order to maintain minimum living standards and to initiate programs designed to rebuild their capital facilities. Crop failures further added to foreign requirements in the short run. With the U. S. Government financing these requirements on a large scale, the demand for our exports soon rose to a postwar peak not approached in earlier or later peacetime years. . . .

The salient features of this long-term record may be summarized as follows. The $440 billion of gross national output in 1957 compares with an aggregate of $196 billion at the end of the 1920's—the last prewar period of generally prosperous conditions—and with the $112 billion in 1909, these earlier figures also being stated in 1957 prices. Thus, total real output has quadrupled over the last 50 years. This rise represents an average annual growth of about 3 per cent—a rate which held approximately both in the 1909-29 period and in the subsequent 3-decade interval.

With population doubling, per capita output in real terms in 1957 was twice that of 1909.

In a basic sense, the increase in real output was even more pronounced. The available statistical techniques make only partial allowance for changes in the quality—as distinguished from the quantity—of real output. Inasmuch as improvements in product quality have constituted a major avenue of economic progress, the quantitative measures that can be calculated do not reflect the full extent of our economic growth.

The increase in the number of man-hours worked—an average of about 1 per cent per year since 1909—has been a clear-cut factor in the long-term growth of real output. Employment, it may be noted, expanded substantially more over this period—1½ per cent per year. But the average length of the workweek declined sharply, as employees and entrepreneurs chose to take some of the improvement in their living standards in the form of shorter working hours.

All of the other factors that—in addition to man-hours worked—have contributed to the growth of real output are summed up in a conventional statistical calculation—"output per man-hour worked." This measure has increased at an average annual rate of about 2 per cent over the last half century, thus accounting for the larger part of real output expansion.

Most of this gain has come from technological and managerial progress, a high rate of capital formation including the development of natural resources, and constant ad-

vances in the education and skills of the working population. Shifting of the work force into activities in which
productivity is relatively high has also contributed. So
have the economies of large-scale production and increased
division of labor associated with the growth of population
and of the market economy.

It is not possible to quantify in a comprehensive manner
these manifold factors which have contributed to economic
growth. However, significant measures are available of
one of them—the stock of tangible capital assets used in
the Nation's productive establishments. These show a
striking secular growth in the amount of plant and equipment used per unit of labor engaged in production, and
corroborate the view that this growth is one of the major
factors explaining the rise in the productivity of American
business. . . .

From the standpoint of the present discussion, the most
important facts brought out by this study are those relating to the relative use of labor and capital in manufacturing. Over the last 30 years, the physical amount of capital
applied in manufacturing production virtually doubled,
whereas the number of man-hours worked increased by
two-fifths. In other words, over this period the amount of
capital per man-hour increased more than one-third. This
increased application of capital of improved efficiency undoubtedly has been a big factor in the growth of manufacturing production, which in 1957 had risen to 2½ times its
1929 volume.

The fact that the expansion of output in manufacturing
significantly outstripped that in either labor or capital in-
put underscores the importance of the other factors, noted
above, making for production growth—factors which cannot be quantified.

MARKET DEMAND PATTERNS

Ours is a market economy. Basic to its organization is
a reliance on countless transactions among a multiplicity
of independent economic units to produce and distribute
the Nation's output. Even Government, which has come
to play such a vital role, works its economic influence by
entering the market and by modifying, rather than replac-

ing, market forces. To understand the functioning of the economy, it is necessary to reduce the voluminous detail of business activity to manageable proportions. National income statistics perform this essential task—by delineating the broad markets for national output and the significant types of product and income flows that picture their dimensions and behavior. . . .

A major element of strength in the postwar economy was provided by consumer demand for goods and services. The basic support for this demand stemmed from the dynamic elements in the economy which produced a generally high and expanding flow of income to individuals.

Personal income—which measures this flow on a before-tax basis—totaled $348 billion in 1957 as compared with $192 billion 10 years earlier. This expansion of four-fifths was similar to that in the current-dollar value of gross national product.

Personal income consists in the main of individuals' earnings from current production. A significant additional part is disbursed by government in the form of social security benefits and other transfer payments; these are partly offset by the contributions made by individuals to the financing of the government-administered social insurance programs.

These government payments and social-security deductions made a sizable addition, on balance, to the current purchasing power of consumers in the postwar period. This was more than offset, however, by higher taxes. Income and other tax payments made by individuals to the Federal, State, and local governments in 1957 came to nearly $43 billion, or 12½ per cent of total personal income. This tax ratio varied between 11½ per cent and 12½ per cent from 1951 to 1957, and for the earlier postwar years averaged somewhat lower. In the prewar period, personal taxes had absorbed about 3 per cent of personal income.

With the proportion of income taken by taxes not varying substantially over most of the postwar period, the course of income after taxes paralleled generally that of total personal income. The 1947-57 expansion in disposable personal income likewise approximated four-fifths in dollar terms, and amounted to almost 50 per cent on a real basis

—that is, after allowance for the 10-year increase in consumer prices.

After the end of the war, individuals stepped up their buying relative to income in the attempt to fill backlog demands. These were made effective by a greatly improved financial position reflecting both accumulated liquid assets and lowered debts. Consumer expenditures amounted to 97 per cent of disposable personal income in 1947—an exceptionally high ratio which doubtless meant that an unusual number of families drew on their liquid assets to supplement current income.

The spending-income ratio, however, was soon reduced as the special buying needs were met. It averaged 94½ per cent in the 1948-50 period and 92½ per cent from 1951 to 1957. In none of the 7 years of the latter span did the ratio differ from the average by as much as one percentage point.

The ratio of consumer expenditures to disposable income was thus relatively stable during most of the postwar period—a fact supporting the view that income was by far the principal determinant of consumption. This broad generalization in no way minimizes the role of other factors influencing consumer spending, such as the availability and use of consumer credit. They were manifested most clearly in quarterly variations in the income-consumption ratio; their influence in the shaping of short-term business fluctuations will become apparent from the subsequent discussion of postwar business cycles.

Another point may be noted. The comparative stability found in the consumption-income ratio was not displayed by the saving-income ratio; its relative fluctuations were wide even on an annual basis. Since personal saving is the difference between much larger income and consumption totals, movements in these totals having only slight effect on the consumption-income ratio resulted in much sharper relative changes in saving and in the saving-income ratio.

The consumer market throughout the postwar period absorbed around two-thirds of total gross national product. This share was lower than that which prevailed in prosperous prewar years, when three-fourths of total output flowed through consumer channels.

This fundamental change reflected the expansion in the

role of Government resulting primarily from the heightened requirements of national defense, although an increase in civilian-type services rendered by Government was involved also. This shift to Government in the use of current output was accomplished through a considerable step-up in the rates of taxation. The ratio of disposable personal income to GNP was thereby lowered; and, in turn, there was a corresponding reduction in the ratio of consumption to GNP as individuals in the past decade spent and saved roughly the same proportions of their after-tax incomes as they did in the prewar era.

The reduction in the ratio of personal consumption to production has been accompanied by a large expansion in the latter, and the absolute volume of real consumption is currently far above prewar levels. Compared with the late 1920's, it is more than twice as high in the aggregate and 50 per cent greater on a per capita basis.

The cross-currents in consumer markets were many and varied in the postwar period. Out of the myriad developments, however, certain broad patterns emerge. Apart from the fact that they depict a significant aspect of the postwar economy, knowledge of them may contribute background perspective for studies utilizing the individual product detail. . . .

The divergent movements in the shares of services and nondurable goods, it may be added, proceeded more or less steadily on an annual basis throughout the decade, and involved strikingly different percentage changes in these categories of expenditures. From 1947 to 1957, total outlays by consumers for services advanced 107 per cent; those for nondurable goods, 48 per cent. These compare with increases of 72 per cent in total consumption expenditures and 79 per cent in disposable personal income.

These postwar shifts in the goods-services composition of the consumer market can be viewed broadly in one of two ways. On the one hand, they may represent basic tendencies to which trend significance should be accorded, with the changes since 1947 representing a break with previously established patterns. On the other hand, the early postwar distribution of consumer spending may have been shaped in considerable degree by temporary influences, in which case the observed 1947-57 shifts, particularly of services and nondurable goods, would be viewed largely as movements back toward the more basic relationships depicted by the prewar distribution.

The latter view appears valid. The postwar record, it is believed, does not warrant the assumption that over the long run the trends in spending for services and for nondurable goods are markedly different, or that these broad groups of outlays are substantially independent of changes in disposable income. Supply and price conditions in the consumer market of 1947 were distorted not only by special aftermath-of-war circumstances, but also by carryover effects of the war and depression. In large degree, developments in the ensuing decade reflected a correction of these dislocations.

In an evaluation of the changes in the goods-services distribution of consumer expenditures over the past decade, it should first be noted that they mainly reflected differential price movements rather than fundamental alterations of the consumption pattern in real terms. As Table 1 shows, the 1947 distribution appears much less out of line with 1929 and 1957 when the comparison is based on expenditure data adjusted for changes in prices. Relative to 1929 and 1957, the 1947 share of services is higher in the constant-dollar distribution than it is in the current-dollar figures, and the share of nondurable goods is correspondingly reduced. Some reduction is also apparent in the 1947 ratio of durables to total real spending, indicating that prices of such goods in that year were also relatively high.

Prices of commodities dropped more than those of services in the early 1930's and rose much more from then until shortly after the war, at which time they were substantially higher, relative to 1929, than service prices. The gap between service and commodity prices narrowed substantially in the past decade. . . . Prices of services moved up 40 per cent, or more than double the increase for commodities. Despite these changes, the composite implicit price index for services in 1957 was still up less from 1929 than commodities—60 per cent as compared with 77 per cent.

The steep advance in the dollar value of service expenditures from 1947 to 1957, and the lesser rise of commodities (especially of nondurables), thus reflected primarily a catching-up of the prices of services with those of commodities. This process was fairly pervasive among the major types of expenditures, but developments relating to housing, food, and clothing had a large weight in determining the broad picture of price and volume changes in the consumer market. . . .

Government has provided a large and somewhat irregular market for the Nation's output in the postwar period. Total purchases of goods and services by Federal, State, and local governments ranged from a low of 12 per cent of GNP in 1947 to a high of 23 per cent in 1953. Recently, about 20 per cent of total output was bought by government.

Changes in the rate of government spending have tended to be concentrated in relatively brief periods. Much of the upward movement to the 1953 high occurred during 1951 and 1952, and the subsequent downward adjustment was accomplished by 1955.

The relative rise in public purchases as compared with the prewar period has been substantial, and has in the main reflected the requirements of national defense. Government purchases for civilian functions have expanded only moderately in relation to total output. Changes in the defense program have been the main source also of the postwar fluctuations of government spending.

National defense purchases—$44 billion in 1957—consist mainly of expenditures for the military functions of the Defense Department. Also included are goods destined for military assistance to foreign countries, outlays for atomic energy development and the stockpiling of strategic and critical materials. Since 1953, and over the postwar decade as a whole, defense outlays have accounted for about one-half of total governmental purchases. Their share was lower prior to the Korean war, and higher during the years of that conflict.

Dollarwise, and also in percentage terms, fluctuations have been particularly pronounced in the procurement of military equipment, currently the largest single item in a broad object breakdown of defense outlays. Moreover, the composition of equipment procurement has been subject to continuing change, as rapid progress in military

TABLE 1

PER CENT DISTRIBUTIONS OF CONSUMER EXPENDITURES
BY MAJOR GROUPS, IN CURRENT AND CONSTANT DOLLARS

	Distribution based on current dollars			Distribution based on constant (1957) dollars			Implicit price deflators (1957 = 100)		
	1929	1947	1957	1929	1947	1957	1929	1947	1957
Total goods and services	100.0	100.0	100.0	100.0	100.0	100.0	58	80	100
Durable goods.....	11.7	12.4	14.0	11.7	11.8	14.0	58	85	100
Nondurable goods....	47.7	56.5	48.5	50.2	53.2	48.5	55	85	100
Food and beverages	24.7	32.9	26.6	26.1	30.5	26.6	55	87	100
Clothing and shoes	11.9	11.4	8.6	13.5	10.2	8.6	51	89	100
Other.....	11.1	12.2	13.3	10.6	12.5	13.3	61	78	100
Services.....	40.6	31.1	37.5	38.1	35.0	37.5	62	71	100
Housing...	14.5	9.4	12.5	10.0	10.5	12.5	84	72	100
Other.....	26.1	21.7	25.0	28.1	24.5	25.0	54	71	100

technology has led to a high rate of obsolescence in general, and more particularly to a shift from conventional items to nuclear and other modern weapons.

Inasmuch as the production of military goods is concentrated largely in durable goods manufacturing, the impact of changes in the defense program on the national economy cannot be inferred from comparisons of the broad defense and national output totals alone. As the subsequent analysis of postwar business fluctuations will show, the specific industrial incidence of defense purchases is an essential link in the chain of causal events explaining the dynamics of postwar business conditions.

In an assessment of the longer-range economic effects of the defense program, its impact on scientific and technological progress should be noted. The large defense funds now being disbursed for research and development have augmented substantially the total amount of our national resources devoted to this purpose. The direct aim of these public outlays is of course the strengthening of our military defenses, but they also affect general economic productivity because of the close interrelations which have developed between military and industrial technological progress.

As already indicated, purchases for civilian functions have accounted for about one-half of the government total since the war. State and local expenditures have far outranked the nondefense outlays of the Federal Government. Amounting to $13 billion in 1947 and to $36 billion 10 years later, they rose steadily over the entire decade. Federal purchases were about $5 billion in both terminal years, although their decade average was somewhat higher.

The upsurge in State and local purchases—from less than 6 per cent to 8 per cent of GNP—is explicable partly in terms of prior restrictions upon such spending. During the war these restrictions reflected the precedence of military over civilian requirements. In the prewar decade they stemmed mainly from the inpaired fiscal position of State and local government units.

Contrariwise, the generally prosperous conditions of the postwar period improved the revenue sources of State and local governments and their ability to borrow, and otherwise strengthened their willingness to embark upon construction and other programs. Population growth and shifts—such as the movement to suburban residential areas —provided a special impetus to the demand for many services typically provided by these governments.

A detailed view of government services in the national income framework is provided for the first time by the new functional breakdown of public expenditures included in this report. Outlays for education—including new construction as well as running expenses—currently account for almost two-fifths of total State and local purchases. Expenditures for highways (the construction of which is financed to a substantial extent by Federal grants) account for another 20 per cent. The remaining two-fifths implements a wide variety of other functions, the most important of which are health and sanitation, general administration, public safety and protection, the provision of public utility capital facilities, and the maintenance and development of natural resources.

Most of the categories of State and local purchases have shared in the postwar expansion of the total. Inasmuch as a major part of this expansion took the form of new construction, which had lagged particularly in the prior decade, categories of expenditures—such as education and highways—which involve relatively high ratios of new construction grew at particularly rapid rates.

Developments in the area of Federal civilian purchases have been less striking. Examination of the record reveals the increased Federal responsibilities (as compared with the prewar period) in such varied fields as foreign affairs, public health, social security, the care of veterans, transportation, agriculture, and natural resources. But fluctuations in Federal purchasing of sufficient size to make an imprint on overall business conditions have been confined to two major programs: expenditures for agricultural price support mainly by the Commodity Credit Corporation, and (in the earlier part of the decade) foreign economic assistance in kind. . . .

TABLE 2

GOVERNMENT RECEIPTS AND EXPENDITURES
IN THE NATIONAL INCOME ACCOUNTS
SELECTED YEARS, 1929-57
[Billions of dollars]

	1929	1947	1950	1953	1957
Receipts.................	11.3	57.1	69.3	94.9	116.2
Personal taxes.........	2.6	21.5	20.8	35.8	42.7
Corporate profits taxes..	1.4	11.3	17.9	20.2	21.6
Indirect business taxes..	7.0	18.6	23.7	30.2	37.6
Contributions for social insurance............	.2	5.7	6.9	8.7	14.2
Expenditures............	10.2	43.8	61.1	102.0	114.5
Purchases.............	8.5	28.4	39.0	82.8	85.7
National defense.....	.6	10.2	14.1	49.0	43.9
Other...............	7.8	18.1	24.8	33.9	41.8
Transfer payments, etc.	1.7	15.4	22.1	19.2	28.8
Surplus or deficit.........	1.0	13.3	8.2	−7.1	1.7

A few major developments explain the postwar course of these government payments to individuals. Most important was the expansion of the various social security programs broadly defined, which has reflected both natural growth and extended coverage. The old-age and survivors insurance program was the most important item in this connection, accounting for $7 billion of the $9 billion net growth of transfer payments from 1947 to 1957. State unemployment insurance benefit payments have risen also as rates were increased, and so have disbursements for the various forms of public assistance. . . .

Partly countering the growth of these and other civilian types of transfers have been disbursements to former military personnel. Military pensions, disability, and retirement payments increased throughout the postwar period. But their annual growth was more than offset until recently by the progressive decline of special programs—such as mustering-out and terminal leave payments, and readjustment, self-employment, and subsistence allowances to veterans—which were at their peak in the years immediately following World War II.

HIGHER TAX YIELDS

As can be seen from Table 2, the enlarged flow of governmental expenditures during the postwar period was accompanied by a record volume of taxation. Combined receipts of all levels of government in 1957, at $116 billion, about matched expenditures for that year. Individual income and other personal taxes accounted for almost 40 per cent of the receipts aggregate, and corporate profits taxes for almost 20 per cent. Sales, excise, property and other indirect taxes constituted more than 30 per cent of the total, and the remaining 10 per cent consisted of employment taxes and other contributions for social insurance.

In spite of changes in tax rates, these broad proportions are generally representative of the source pattern of governmental receipts for the postwar period as a whole.

The main contrast with the late 1920's lies in the relative expansion of individual and corporate income taxes, which are the mainstays of the expanded Federal revenue structure, and in the employment taxes associated with the social security program which had not been established in the earlier period. Mirroring these developments, the share of indirect taxes has declined. . . .

Foreign Markets.—Exports are another major market for United States production. Foreign demand was high through most of the postwar period. Centering at first on the needs of economic reconstruction, it subsequently reflected the general prevalence of prosperity and the investment programs all over the world which have been aimed at long-run improvement in living standards.

Foreign purchases from the United States are of course financed mainly through foreigners' sales to us. In the postwar period, however, an unusually large fraction of the financing has been dependent on loan and cash aid programs carried on by the United States Government. Outlays under such programs aggregated $30 billion in the 1946-57 period. Adding aid in kind—which, however, is treated in the GNP measures as a component of Government purchases—brings the 12-year total of United States aid to $62 billion.

Loan and grant funds from this country played an especially important part in foreign trade financing under the conditions of economic emergency just after the war. Their relative role has declined since that time, as imports have tended upward with the general economic expansion. While total cash grants and loans under these Government programs have shown no growth in the period, they have been continued on a substantial scale as part of our overall international security program, and are still of critical importance to free economies in many parts of the world.

Foreign countries bought roundly 5 per cent of the postwar output of the United States, the fraction having reached a peak of 8 per cent in 1947. In absolute terms the high point came in 1957, with an export total of $26 billion. (These figures exclude military and other Federal aid in kind.) Though price advances contributed to the growth of the total over the past decade, there was a substantial increase in real volume as well.

Superimposed on the basic tendency of exports to expand since World War II has been a series of large fluctuations. The most notable of these was the bulge which came as an immediate aftermath of the war. Aside from emergency needs for the relief and rehabilitation of foreign nationals at that time, United States products were needed to help make good the destruction or undermaintenance of productive facilities abroad. Many countries, moreover, had accumulated liquid reserves and deferred requirements for United States production, just as had the United States consumer and capital-goods markets.

Subsequent fluctuations around the longer-term uptrend stemmed from a variety of similarly transitory factors. A sharp reaction followed the 1947 peak. Somewhat later, the Korean hostilities had brief but widespread repercussions in world markets. These, like the more limited effects of the Suez crisis of late 1957, were additional to the changes attributable to such factors as year-to-year variations in world output and prices of agricultural commodities, and to cyclical movements in European business activity.

Our figures show how foreign buyers obtained dollar exchange to pay for their purchases of United States products. Since 1947 such buying has totaled close to $200 billion. All but about $30 billion was balanced by United States purchases from abroad. Two-thirds of the remainder was financed through cash grants by the United States Government, and one-third through United States private and public investment.

Imports of goods and services grew rather steadily throughout the period, and in 1957 passed $20 billion—a figure more than twice that recorded a decade earlier. After allowance for the rise in prices, the bulk of this expansion is seen to have reflected an increase in the physical volume of trade.

Dollar earnings of foreigners from sales to the United States tended to finance a progressively larger share of our exports as war-born dislocations were overcome. The export surplus declined from $9 billion in 1947 to $1 billion or less annually in most years of the 1950-55 period. There was, however, an increase in the past 2 years.

From 1952 to 1957, the portion of this surplus financed by cash transfers from the Federal Government was stable at about $1½ billion a year, or roughly half as much as in the peak years of the Marshall Plan. These cash transfers are grants for the furthering of economic development abroad. (Military aid, being given in kind rather than in cash, is excluded here along with economic aid in kind; this treatment is consistent with that underlying the GNP measure of exports.)

Net foreign investment by the United States has been comparatively limited in most years since the early postwar period, when the totals were swelled by Federal Government loans of an emergency aid character. In the 1950-55 period, in fact, foreigners' new investment (including gold purchases) here generally exceeded the flow of United States capital abroad. More recently, there was a rise in net foreign investment by the United States. This involved a sharp expansion in the outflow of American private capital and, in 1957, a drop in new investment here by foreigners. The net effect was to permit the financing of a $4 billion increase in our export balance from 1955 to 1957 with relatively little dependence on expansion in Government grants and lending.

Private investment abroad fluctuated around $1 billion annually during most of the postwar period, but rose in 1956 and 1957 to $3 billion or more. Direct investment of United States business firms in foreign branches and subsidiaries accounted for $2 billion in each of those years.

One of the characteristic features of foreign investment since the war has been the relatively large contribution of direct investment to the total. Ordinary trade-finance credit and the purchase of foreign securities as portfolio investments, on the other hand, have been relatively less important than in prewar patterns of capital outflow.

As has been noted, United States Government programs have released dollar exchange in our foreign markets not only through the cash grants distinguished in the table but also through international loans and credits.

In addition to the foreign purchases of our output which have been made possible with these funds, large amounts of American goods and services have been bought by the Federal Government for the use of friendly foreign nations under our military and economic aid programs. The $62-billion total comprises such assistance in kind as well as loans and cash grants. The great bulk of this total is seen to have taken the form of grants rather than loans. Two-thirds of it was for emergency relief and other economic aid; the military-aid fraction has been up in recent years, however, amounting since 1952 to over one-half of the total.

Domestic Investment.—An essential requirement for a progressive industrial economy is that a portion of current output be used for investment in capital goods. The United States economy has characteristically featured a high rate of investment; this has been a major influence in the outstanding growth of our standard of living.

Investment is typically one of the more dynamic elements of demand. Its principal components—fixed capital and inventories—are both subject to rapid change. The former accounts for the principal share of total investment, and includes outlays on industrial plant and equipment, housing, and related facilities. Since multiple-use goods of relatively long life are involved, production of them need not be geared at all closely to current use, and hence can be bunched or postponed.

Inventory investment—the change in business inventories—is an item which can be either positive or negative as inventories are raised or lowered. It is subject to pronounced short-term variability—a feature brought out in the subsequent discussion of postwar cyclical developments. At this time, however, attention is called to one central fact: Inventory holdings are a sizable element in the capital structure of business, and their expansion with the growth of the economy has accounted for a significant part of total investment. In manufacturing, which holds a large part of all inventory goods in the economy, stocks at the end of 1957 came to over $50 billion, equal to roughly three-eighths of the total of capital goods in the industry. Moreover, the buildup of manufacturers' inventories over the 1929-57 span was nearly as large as the growth in the net real value of structures and equipment.

Gross fixed business investment—expenditures on nonresidential construction and producers' durable equipment—reached $47 billion in 1957, an all-time high in terms of both current dollars and physical volume. This investment was sizable throughout the postwar period, even when reduced during the brief intervals of cyclical contraction.

A large backlog of demand for capital facilities had accumulated by the end of World War II, stemming from the period of underinvestment during the 1930's, restrictions imposed in the war period, and the heavy wear-and-tear on equipment involved in the pressures of war production. Once supply conditions after the war permitted resumption of volume production of capital goods, business moved forward almost continuously in its programs of modernization and expansion, spurred by the general prosperity of the period. These programs traced three wavelike patterns superimposed on an upward sloping trend: the first culminating in 1948, the second in 1953, and the third in 1957.

While the expansion in outlays for business facilities in the postwar period reflected in part rising equipment prices and construction costs, the new additions to the physical stock of capital were of record proportions.

Current-dollar outlays in this period constituted about the same relative share of GNP—around one-tenth—as in the prosperous 1920's, the most recent comparable period of facilities expansion. Expressed in constant dollars, the share of postwar fixed investment was somewhat lower than in that earlier period. However, it seems best not to read this difference too literally, inasmuch as the constant-dollar data do not take complete account of quality change and over the long-run quality improvements in fixed equipment probably have exceeded those in other goods and services.

Ratios of fixed investment to total output, while helpful in studying market demand patterns and fluctuations, do not portray the extent to which the supply of capital is geared to growth requirements. To shed light on this latter aspect, information on productive capacity is needed. While this is difficult to obtain, a few broad qualitative aspects may be noted in assessing the postwar investment programs of business.

The first relates to the environment in which the postwar expansion was initiated and carried through. While private investment was held back in the 1930's and the war years, advances in science and technology had continued apace. The intensive search for labor- and materials-saving facilities encouraged by the pressures of war requirements, and the subsequent continuing emphasis on research and development, quickened the pace of discovery of new techniques. Thus, it was possible to incorporate into the postwar programs types of machinery, materials, and processes which were probably far more efficient than ever before.

Secondly, it appears that the capital stock in the past decade was in an especially favorable working condition in terms of its age composition. To throw some light on the "newness" aspect of facilities, an attempt has been made to measure the relation of net equipment stocks (after depreciation) to gross stocks. Whereas this ratio will tend to exceed 50 per cent in a growing economy, throughout most of the period it was markedly above it, and exceeded the 55 per cent ratio which applied during the late 1920's.

A third factor to be noted about postwar business fixed investment concerns its relative composition as between equipment and construction: This differed markedly from that of the 1920's. [According to] the shift, . . . business expenditures for fixed capital in the recent period were concentrated much more heavily upon acquisition of new equipment, and proportionately less upon plant expansion. . . .

In addition to the substantial accumulation of industry-type fixed facilities during the past decade, investment in new housing for the Nation's population also represented an important claim on resources and at the same time contributed significantly to the favorable record of total business activity.

Nonfarm residential construction amounted to $17 billion in 1957. This was moderately below the record of $18½ billion in 1955, but almost 2½ times the dollar volume of 1947 which was still affected by conditions carrying over from the war. Much of this dollar rise over the decade represented higher construction costs; after allowance for this factor, the real volume of nonfarm housing put in place in 1957 was half again as large as in the earlier year.

During the first few years after World War II, demands for housing associated with normal family growth were augmented by demands of many families which had been required to "double-up" because of war-engendered shortages or still inadequate financial resources. Thus, demand was strong; the ceiling on housing activity was set by the capacity limitations of the period.

By the early 1950's, these abnormal demand and supply conditions had been substantially alleviated. Construction of new housing was exceptionally rapid in 1950, with the physical volume put in place that year up almost 40 per cent over the average of the two preceding years. The volume of activity tapered in 1951 and 1952, rose to an all-time high by 1955, and receded over the next two years. The quantity of housing put in place in 1957 equaled that of 1950, and was higher than in any prior year.

For the postwar period as a whole, the absolute volume of housing production was far above any previous experience. Relative to the total value of output, nonfarm residential construction was close to that of the 1920's, which encompassed the previous housing boom.

A combination of favorable circumstances helped to make effective the record housing requirements of the postwar period. Incomes were high and generally rising; other financial circumstances of would-be homeowners, including their liquid-asset position, were also generally favorable; and the terms of financing were made more liberal than ever before.

As the postwar experience unfolded, mortgage financing terms became a significant factor influencing housing activity. Liberalization of terms helped the expansion of residential purchases in 1949-50, in 1954-55, and probably in 1957-58. On the other hand, in 1951-52 and 1956-57 changes in mortgage terms appear to have constituted restrictive influences.

The tremendous volume of postwar investment entailed financing on an unprecedented scale.

For the economy as a whole, the saving required to finance the expansion of capital assets is derived from individuals, corporations, and government. . . .

. . . private domestic investment dominates the overall investment picture. Foreign investment for the 1947-57 period taken as a whole amounted to only 2 per cent of a gross investment aggregate on the order of $575 billion.

On the saving side, perhaps the most noteworthy feature revealed by the consolidated statement is that private saving—from individuals and corporations—accounted for all but a small fraction of the postwar total. The portion of total national saving contributed by government—through an excess of governmental receipts over expenditures—

was less than 5 per cent for the 1947-57 period as a whole.

As pointed out earlier, the cumulative governmental surplus on income and product transactions for this period amounted to $26 billion—comprised of a surplus of $30 billion for the Federal Government and a deficit of $4 billion for State and local governments. On a year-to-year basis, it may be emphasized again, swings in the government surplus or deficit were sometimes sizable; they affected short-run economic developments much more than is indicated by the cumulative data which are used to provide a broad postwar perspective. . . .

In the acquisition of tangible assets, the major use of individuals' capital funds in the postwar period was for investment in housing. The remainder of physical investments made by individuals—also large—was in their capacity as owners of noncorporate businesses, and consisted primarily of outlays for fixed facilities.

The investment of nonfarm entrepreneurs involved in opening new businesses was an especially dynamic factor in the early postwar years. The business population had been restricted during the depression and the war, but with the return to prosperous peacetime conditions new firms were formed at a record rate. By 1948 the business population was restored to a size more in line with the long-term trend.

Individuals channeled a sizable share of their gross saving into the more liquid types of assets in the past decade. About $75 billion was added to cash and savings accounts, or two-fifths of individuals' total addition to financial assets. This was superimposed on the already huge accumulations built up during the war. When individuals are considered as a group, their liquid-asset position was quite favorable throughout the postwar period, far more so than before the war.

Individuals also added around $70 billion to their equities in private insurance and pension reserves. The funds thus set aside were, of course, available through financial intermediaries for financing the capital requirements of business firms and purchasers of other capital assets, such as housing. A sizable additional volume of saving in the form of insurance and pension reserves accrued to individuals through government-administered funds; such saving, as already noted, is regarded in the national accounts as part of the government surplus.

The remainder of the financial asset accumulation of individuals took the form of purchases of securities, divided about equally between government and private issues. These purchases either represented a direct contribution of individuals to the financing of the issuing units or were an addition to the indirect supply of personal saving which flowed through banks and other financial institutions to the investment markets.

These accumulations of physical and financial assets by individuals were financed from gross saving and from borrowed funds roughly in a 2-to-1 proportion. The postwar rise in individuals' indebtedness, about $170 billion, was exceptionally rapid. This is explained in part by the relatively low indebtedness at the end of World War II. The favorable wartime financial conditions had permitted most individuals to pay off a substantial amount of outstanding debt; at the same time, wartime restrictions had limited the availability of housing and consumer durables, the principal uses which normally involve substantial borrowing.

Use of borrowed funds was also fostered by financial developments in the postwar period. Interest costs were low by historical standards, and other terms of borrowing, especially for residential purchases, were greatly liberalized. The largest share of the total increase in personal debt took the form of federally insured or guaranteed mortgages on which terms of financing were especially liberal. Undoubtedly, these permitted the purchase of residential properties by many individuals who might not otherwise have aspired to home ownership. . . .

As in the case of individuals, corporations added substantially to their financial as well as physical assets in the postwar period.

. . . total use of funds requiring financing amounted to about $380 billion. Of this, three-fourths represented investment in tangible assets; one-fourth, an increase in financial assets taking the form of extension in book credit to customers and additions to liquid and other short-term assets.

Note should be taken of the fact that corporations made only slight additions to their liquid resources over the past decade. This reflects for the most part the excess liquidity with which corporate business entered the postwar period. This favorable position was fairly general among business firms, and seldom if ever in the past decade was liquidity an important independent factor serving to limit business activity.

Internal sources—retained earnings and depreciation allowances—accounted for three-fifths of total corporate financial requirements. It may be noted, however, that whereas retained earnings constituted the predominant form of internal financing in the early part of the decade, the steady rise of depreciation made that source of financing predominant in the more recent period.

The reduction in the relative importance of retained earnings was characteristic of most industries, and reflected in considerable degree a gradual move away from the low ratios of dividends to after-tax profits. While these stemmed in part from heavy investment requirements, they were also a legacy of the financial troubles of the 1930's, as most corporate executives carried over at least into the early postwar years a determination to establish comfortable equity cushions.

The almost continuous prosperity of the past decade and its concurrent rebuilding of plant and equipment slowly brought a higher payout to stockholders. However, as late as 1957 the dividend-earnings ratios of most industries remained conservative in historical perspective. These relatively low postwar dividend payments permitted a substantial buildup of equity funds to offset in part the impact on corporation financial structures of the rapid upsurge in postwar borrowing.

The reduced share of retained earnings in gross corporate saving also reflected the substantial and steady postwar rise in depreciation allowances which was general throughout corporate industry. This rise stemmed from both basic factors and from special influences related to tax law changes. Depreciation allowances were fairly low at the start of the period. As the record-breaking postwar spending programs proceeded—generally involving expanded physical capacity purchased at rising cost—the depreciable asset base and depreciation allowances were steadily increased.

Rapid amortization provisions were introduced into the tax laws, first in 1950 for defense-related expansions and later, in 1954, for all new facilities. Both of these changes gave a special impetus to depreciation allowances in the more recent period. By 1957, the 1950 provision was of declining importance, but this was still being largely offset by the rise imparted by the 1954 change. Obviously, as time goes on these special aspects will lose force since there was no change in total depreciation allowed, but merely in its time-phasing.

In addition to the huge amounts of gross equity funds supplied from these internal sources, corporations raised about $25 billion through the sale of new stock issues. These were probably of somewhat lesser relative importance than in earlier prosperous periods, but total equity financing—internal and external combined—appears to have supplied a relatively large part of aggregate needs.

Corporate business borrowed substantial sums in the postwar period, with the net increase in interest-bearing debt from 1947 to 1957 amounting to $60 billion.

In consideration of this increase, it should be noted first that debt and its servicing requirements were exceptionally low at the start of the period. Not only had corporations paid off a substantial volume of existing obligations from liquid funds accumulated during the war years, but much of the debt still outstanding had been refinanced on the more favorable terms then prevailing. . . .

CHANGING INCOME STRUCTURE

The expansion of gross national product has been accompanied by a corresponding rise in the national income —a comprehensive alternative measure of national output expressed in terms of the earnings derived from production. From 1947 to 1957, the national income increased from $198 billion to $364 billion, or four-fifths. This rise, of course, reflected not only the expansion in physical volume of production but also the sharp advance in prices over the period.

Interest attaches to the national income mainly because it lends itself to breakdowns which differ from those of the gross national product, and hence throw additional light on the functioning of the economy.

In this section, the broad effects of changes in the product composition of output on the industrial income structure are traced, and it is shown how changes in that structure, in turn, influenced the forms—such as wages and profits—in which income has accrued. Industrial shifts affect the forms of income mainly because the various industries differ widely as to their predominant type of legal organization—e.g., corporate vs. noncorporate business—and hence as to the income type patterns they generate.

Analysis of these basic distributions of income—by industry, by type, and by legal form of organization—is of interest primarily because they provide essential links in explaining the circular flow of income and purchasing power through the economy as this is affected by, and in turn affects, final demand as registered in the GNP. . . .

In the conventional breakdown of gross national product by type of expenditures, the goods-services classification is provided only for the consumer market, and, in the case of construction, only the private component is shown. The new table extends the goods-services-construction breakdown to the entire GNP. It provides a superior basis for studying the link between product demand and industrial activity, since the industrial structure of national income is closely related to this comprehensive product classification of total output. . . .

Over the past decade, the principal change in composition of gross national product was a relative decline in the goods portion and a rise in the services portion. This is evident from the following data:

	Per cent of GNP.		
	1929	1947	1957
Goods...................	54	61	53
Services.................	35	31	35
Construction............	11	8	12

This shift from 1947 to 1957 does not appear to have been part of a long-run trend. When the figures are considered in historical perspective, and interpreted in light of the particular economic forces at work in the early postwar period, the goods-services-construction break-down of GNP for 1947 appears out of line. Specifically, the goods component seems relatively high, and services and construction correspondingly low. From this vantage point, the postwar shifts in broad product composition are seen to have represented a return toward earlier, more normal patterns, rather than the establishment of new basic movements and relationships. This generalization is similar to that already made in the case of personal consumption, which, of course, is a major determinant of the product composition of GNP.

When durable goods and nondurable goods are looked at separately, it is clear that the up-then-down pattern of the total goods percentage reflects the movement of non-durable goods, which are the larger part of the total. The durable goods percentage for 1947 did not differ substantially from what would have been expected on the basis of the apparent long-term upward trend in the relative importance of durable goods in the gross national product. . . .

The effect of this pattern on the industrial origin of national income is clearly evident when the separate industry divisions are grouped according to whether their output is mainly dependent, directly or indirectly, on final demand for goods and construction, on the one hand, or for services, on the other. Needless to say, such a grouping of industries must be somewhat arbitrary. Many industries contribute to the final value of both goods and services. The transportation industry is an example. Transportation services enter the value of goods output in the GNP and are also represented directly as services when bought separately by final users, as in the case of the transportation of passengers.

For purpose of the present analysis, the goods-associated industries are considered to be agriculture, manufacturing, mining, contract construction, trade, and transportation; the services-associated industries consist of finance, communications and public utilities, services proper, and government.

The contract construction industry is not classified

separately by reason of the fact that there is only tenuous correspondence in movement between this industry on the income side and construction activity as included in the GNP. Among the several differences in coverage between the two measures, most important are these: That the GNP construction component—unlike the contract construction industry—includes force-account work and excludes altogether the value of maintenance and repair. In the text table below, construction is included with goods in both the GNP and national income breakdowns:

	1929	1947	1957
Goods (including construction) as per cent of GNP.........	65	69	65
Goods-associated industries as per cent of NI.............	64	70	64
Services as per cent of GNP...	35	31	35
Services-associated industries as per cent of NI..........	36	30	36

As may be seen, there is a remarkable correspondence between the goods and services breakdowns of the gross national product and national income. While this may have stemmed in part from offsetting errors in the income allocations, the tabulation establishes beyond doubt the pervasive influence of shifts in the composition of final demand on the postwar industrial income structure. This influence, it may be added, is evident not only in the above comparison involving the years 1947 and 1957, but on an annual basis as well. Clearly depicted by the annual data is a more or less steady rise in the services share of both GNP and national income, and a corresponding reduction in the share of these aggregates accounted for by goods.

Since the postwar shifts in product composition of GNP reflected in the main relatively short-term adjustments, rather than basic trends, the same generalization applies to the income changes which they produced. This central finding should serve as a background in more detailed studies of the postwar industrial origin of national income.

The breakdowns of GNP shown above are based on the current-dollar values of goods and services. If analogous breakdowns of constant-dollar GNP are prepared, the relative shares of goods and services in 1947 appear to be fairly well in line with long-run developments. In other words, the postwar shifts in product composition of GNP were due mainly to the price factor—to relatively high prices for goods and low prices for services in 1947, and to their subsequent readjustment. Therefore, it seems evident that measures of real income or output by industry would show developments for the postwar period much more in conformity with long-term trends than those displayed by the current-dollar data analyzed above.

While any detailed examination of individual industries is precluded, it will be of interest to highlight the main developments which occurred in farming, manufacturing, trade, and government. The first three account for the bulk of the goods-associated industry group. Government forms a significant part of the services-associated group, and is of independent interest. With respect to the private-industry components of the latter group, it may be noted that their rate of increase over the postwar period generally exceeded that of total national income. This uniformity of developments reflected the broad supply and demand conditions which in the past decade affected the services area of the economy as a whole.

Income originating in farming has had a long-term downtrend relative to total national income. In the early postwar period, however, farming temporarily regained a share of the income total—nearly 10 per cent—matching that of the late 1920's. This experience was due to the prevailing relatively high prices for farm products which reflected a strong domestic market reinforced by exceptional foreign demand. The latter, as noted earlier, was an outcome of the damaged state of world agriculture and of the poor growing conditions abroad which characterized the early postwar years.

As world crop and livestock conditions improved, farm prices began to recede, and the longer-term trends affecting United States farm income reappeared. Beginning with 1949, income from farming declined steadily as a proportion of the national income, to a figure of 4 per cent in 1957.

Though the farm share of total national income has

fallen sharply, per capita income originating in farming
has been well maintained over the past quarter-century in
relation to the all-industry average. Underlying this development is a strong shift of labor away from farming; the
number of persons engaged in this industry declined from
19 per cent of all persons engaged in production in 1929
to 8 per cent in 1957.

Manufacturing, the largest of the goods-associated industries, increased greatly in relative importance from
1929 to 1957—from 25 per cent to 31 per cent of the national income. A figure similar to that for 1957 had been
established by 1947 and, with irregular variations, was
characteristic of the entire postwar decade.

The trend significance of this stability—its meaning for
the longer run—is quite uncertain because of the many
special factors that were operative in this comparatively
brief period. Important among them were the abnormally
high output of goods in the early postwar years, to which
manufacturing was the major contributor; the particular
impact of the Korean conflict upon this industry; and the
three postwar recessions which, although mild for the
economy as a whole, significantly affected the course of
production in manufacturing. While measurement is not
possible, it would seem that up through the Korean conflict
the net balance of economic forces was especially favorable
for the manufacturing industry; one should therefore not
conclude that the postwar stability in the ratio of manufacturing to total national income rules out the presence of
an underlying upward trend.

Income originating in trade is strongly correlated with
demand for goods, and followed quite closely the post-1947
decline in the ratio of goods output to total production.
Trade income rose from 15 per cent of the national income
total in 1929 to 19 per cent in 1947—then declined to 16
per cent in 1957. This postwar decline was broken only by
slight rises in 1949 and 1954 as income from trade in
those years weakened less than income from manufacturing
and certain other industries particularly affected by the
recessions.

Income originating in government—the compensation
of government employees (including military personnel)—
accounted for 9 per cent of the national income in 1947. It

moved up irregularly to 12 per cent of the total by 1952, and held approximately at that figure through 1957. . . .

POSTWAR CYCLICAL DEVELOPMENTS

While one of the outstanding features of the postwar period has been the vigorous uptrend in business activity, the economy has been subject to periods of cyclical fluctuations with recessions occurring in 1948-49, 1953-54, and 1957-58.

These recessions were mild. There was no repetition of the serious cyclical disturbance which ensued shortly after World War I, when total output dropped by 9 per cent from 1920 to 1921, manufacturing activity was off by 25 per cent in the same period, and unemployment in the latter year averaged over 10 per cent of the labor force. The postwar recessions were rather of the same order as the more moderate contractions of the 1910's and 1920's, and substantially milder than the downturn in 1937-38 when the economy moved sharply lower despite the incomplete nature of the previous recovery from the deep 1930-32 depression. . . .

The spread between the current-dollar and constant-dollar values of gross national product reflects, of course, the advance in prices which prevailed over much of the postwar period, and which made for a generally more pronounced upward movement in the current-dollar line. The impact of inflation was largest in the years immediately after the war, when controls were lifted and costs and prices were brought into a new alignment. More than one-half of the entire postwar price increase occurred in the 1946-48 period, when extraordinary demands placed a severe strain on productive capacity.

The postwar period featured two other pronounced upward movements in prices. One was associated with the Korean conflict; the other occurred during 1956 and 1957 . . . comparative stability prevailed in the period 1952-55, although the general average of GNP prices edged upward. This experience reflected the better adaptation of supply to demand after the Korean buildup, as discussed later; the dampening effects of the 1953-54 downturn; and the offsetting movements during the period in the agricultural and industrial components entering the final price structure. By early 1956, agricultural as well as other prices were on the upgrade in a general setting of buoyant demand, high output, and rising production costs.

It is noteworthy that in the past decade there was an almost total absence of downward pressures on the general price level. Even in the two most recent recessions, prices edged forward. A moderate downward movement was registered in the 1948-49 period concurrent with the break in agricultural prices in early 1948. . . .

Index, peak-output quarter=100

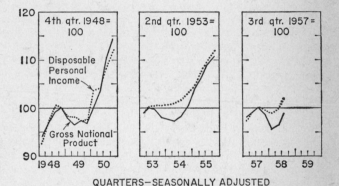

QUARTERS—SEASONALLY ADJUSTED

CONSUMER BUYING POWER BETTER
MAINTAINED THAN OUTPUT DURING
POSTWAR RECESSIONS

THE BALANCE SHEET OF AGRICULTURE, 1960[26]

It was not until the appearance of Lend-Lease in 1940 that farm income began to rise; and it has continued to do so. Nevertheless, the surpluses also have remained, and every effort to cope with them has led to frustration and failure. Government payments to farmers were $723 million in 1940, $1,089 million in 1958, and $681 million in 1959.

✓   ✓   ✓

The total value of farm assets rose to a new record level in the 12 months ending January 1, 1960. Over the same period, however, farm operators' net realized income from farming dropped from the relatively high level of 1958 to a level approximating the average for 1955-57.

Although the average income per person on farms from farming and off-farm sources was lower in 1959 than in 1958, it was higher than for any other year since 1951. Over this period, more and more farm families have been supplementing their farm income by obtaining off-farm jobs. At the same time, the number of farms has been decreasing and farm income has been distributed among fewer people.

Farms assets on January 1, 1960, were valued at $203.6 billion, less than 1 per cent above a year earlier. The increase of $1.3 billion in such assets during 1959 contrasted with increases of about $8 billion in 1956, $10 billion in 1957, and $16 billion in 1958.

Farm debts continued to be small relative to farm assets. On January 1, 1960, debts totaled $24.3 billion, about 12 per cent of the value of farm assets. The equities of farm-

[26] *Federal Reserve Bulletin* (August, 1960), pp. 848-851.

ers and other owners of farm property remained virtually unchanged at the record level of about $179 billion in 1959, in contrast with increases of $7.6 billion, $9.0 billion, and $13.2 billion, respectively, during the preceding three years.

Real estate—the principal farm asset—rose about $4 billion in value in 1959. This was a substantial increase but less than in any of the preceding three years. Further increases also occurred in the value of farm machinery and motor vehicles, of household furnishings and equipment, and of farmers' investments in cooperatives. But the value of both crop and livestock inventories declined, and, for the first time in 10 years, farmers' holdings of deposits and currency were reduced substantially. . . .

Farmer-owned inventories of crops were nearly 15 per cent lower in value on January 1, 1960, than a year earlier, chiefly because of a change in the cotton price-support program and a smaller wheat crop in 1959. The 1959 cotton crop was supported chiefly through direct purchases by the Commodity Credit Corporation rather than through loan operations. . . .

Farm machinery and motor vehicles on farms increased in value by about $700 million during 1959. Expenditures for these items exceeded depreciation charges, but most of the rise in inventory values was the result of a revaluation of the inventory at the higher prices prevailing at the end of 1959.

Farm debts increased by only about 4 per cent during 1959 compared with an increase of nearly 15 per cent in 1958. The difference between the two years in over-all debt growth reflected a decline in 1959 in price-support loans of the Commodity Credit Corporation.

Farm mortgage debt increased by about 9 per cent during 1959, compared with about 7 per cent in 1958. The non-real estate farm debt, excluding Commodity Credit Corporation loans, increased by about 12 per cent, the same as in 1958. The continued growth in these types of debt reflects the increase in credit-financed transfers of farm real estate and the rising level of farm expenditures for production and capital equipment. However, farm debts remain relatively small and farm foreclosures and distress transfers continue near a record low. . . .

PHYSICAL ASSETS OF AGRICULTURE VALUED AT 1940 PRICES,
UNITED STATES, JANUARY 1, 1940, AND 1960

Type	Amount (in billions of dollars)		Net increase (per cent)
	1940	1960	1940-60
Real estate.................	33.6	38.2	13.6
Livestock..................	5.1	5.3	3.2
Machinery and motor vehicles	3.1	7.3	137.9
Crops stored on and off farms	2.7	3.8	43.4
Household furnishings and equipment..............	4.3	7.2	69.2
Total..................	48.8	61.8	26.8

The slowing down of the growth in farm assets and
equities and the decline in farm incomes occurred in spite
of high and rising general economic activity. Total output
of goods and services, which continued its recovery from
the 1958 recession, gained rapidly in the first half of 1959
and reached a record $488 billion rate in the April-June
quarter. Work stoppages after midyear caused some decline in gross national product, but final purchases continued upward throughout the year. For the year as a
whole gross national product averaged $482 billion, 8.5
per cent over 1958.

Employment also set new records. With widespread expansion in both hourly earnings and the average workweek, wage and salary income showed a gain of almost 8
per cent over 1958.

High levels of employment and income in 1959 supported a strong domestic demand for agricultural products.
Consumer expenditures for food (including alcoholic bev-
erages) increased 1.5 per cent over 1958 to $68.6 billion.
Agricultural exports also increased during the year. Despite this high level of demand, markets for farm products
continued to be dominated by heavy supplies, with the
result that prices trended downward throughout most of
1959.

Increases in the general price level—an important influence on values of farm real estate and other farm assets in recent years—were very small in 1959. But strong demand for credit by business, consumers, and government alike, accompanied by Federal Reserve policies of continued restraint on the growth of the money supply, kept financial markets tight during 1959 and led to further increases in interest rates. Higher costs and limited availability of funds may have been a factor in holding the rise in farm debt (other than to the Commodity Credit Corporation) to about the same as that for 1959.

Gross farm income of $38 billion in 1959 was 3 per cent less than in 1958. Production costs (other than wages, rent, and interest) increased almost 5 per cent to a high of $21.6 billion. With a decrease in gross farm income and an increase in production costs, net income from agriculture dropped about 12 per cent to $16.3 billion.

The net income of farm operators was 16 per cent less in 1959 than in 1958. Omitting adjustments for changes in inventory, the realized net income of farmers dropped to $11.3 billion, or almost 13 per cent. The average realized net income per farm, including farms of all sizes, declined from $2,733 in 1958 to $2,437 in 1959 after allowing for a decrease in the number of farms.

The total volume of farm products sold or used in the home increased 3 per cent from 1958 to 1959 but prices received for those sold declined an average of 4 per cent. The volume of crops sold increased less than 1 per cent and the prices received for crops remained the same as a year earlier. The volume of livestock and livestock products sold increased about 5 per cent but their average prices decreased about 6 per cent.

The purchasing power of the realized net income of farm operators from farming was slightly more than 13 per cent lower in 1959 than in 1958 and was at the same level as 1957. This resulted chiefly from a decline in current dollar income but partly from an increase in prices farmers paid for items used in family living.

Farmers' income from nonfarm sources in 1959 is estimated at $6.8 billion, about 6 per cent more than in 1958. Per capita income of farm people from nonfarm sources increased from $299 in 1958 to a record high of $321 in 1959.

— 27 —

THE ECONOMY AT THE OPENING OF 1961 [27]

The advisers of President-elect John F. Kennedy were less sanguine about the American economy in 1961 than had been the Department of Commerce in 1958. On January 5, 1961, a report, written by Professor Paul A. Samuelson of the Massachusetts Institute of Technology and entitled "Prospects and Policies for the 1961 American Economy," was released. The Report called attention to the fact that the recovery from the recession of 1957-58 had not been as complete as had been supposed, and that, with the second quarter of 1960, the economy had begun to slip again. The Report proposed certain short-term measures to speed recovery. All were familiar; indeed they had been used, in one form or another, during the recessions of 1948-49, 1953-54, and 1957-58. The Report had nothing to say about these long-term factors that had been slowing down American growth from 1956 on—at the very time that the Russian economy was showing such phenomenal advances. Professor Samuelson, at the very end, admits "that there are some problems that fiscal and monetary policy cannot themselves come to grips with"; and says, without indicating lines of policy himself, "What may then be needed are new approaches to the problem of productivity, wages, and price formation." For a discussion of the general problem of growth, in the light of what happened in 1960, see Louis M. Hacker, "The New Decade: An Interim Report" in the Saturday Review, *February 4, 1961, pp. 10-13, 48.*

[27] Reprinted in newspapers, January 6, 1961.

I. THE ECONOMIC OUTLOOK

1. *Recession.* Economic experts are generally agreed that the nation's economy is now in a "recession." The slide since mid-1960 cannot be termed a "depression" like that after 1929, but so widespread a decline in production deserves more than the euphemism of a "rolling readjustment."

Prudent economic policy must face the fact that we go into 1961 with business still moving downward. This means that unemployment, now above 6 per cent of the labor force, may this winter rise more than seasonally. It means still lower profits ahead.

The fact of recession also has significant implications for the prospective budget. It means a falling off of tax receipts from earlier estimated levels. This recession is wiping out the previously estimated budget surplus for the fiscal year ending June 30. Many experts now believe that, as of today, it is reasonable to forecast a deficit for this fiscal year, assuming only expenditures already authorized and in the absence of desirable new expenditures from an accelerated effort. Recalling the experience of the 1957-58 recession may be useful: Due largely to the impact of a recession that everyone but the authorities admitted was then taking place, the announcement in early 1958 of a small fiscal 1959 budget surplus was actually followed by a final fiscal 1959 budget deficit of more than $12,000,000,-000! Not even the ostrich can avert the economic facts of life. He misreads the role of confidence in economic life who thinks that denying the obvious will cure the ailments of a modern economy.

No one can know exactly when this fourth postwar recession will come to an end. A careful canvass of expert opinion and analysis of the economic forces making for further contraction suggest this probability.

With proper actions by the Government, the contraction in business can be brought to a halt within 1961 itself and converted into an upturn. Recognizing that many analysts hope the upturn may come by the middle of the year but recalling how subject to error were their rosy forecasts for 1960, policy makers realize the necessity for preparing to take actions that might be needed if this fourth recession turns out to be a more serious one than its predecessors.

2. *Chronic Slackness*. In economics, the striking event drives out attention from the less-dramatic but truly more fundamental processes. More fraught with significance for public policy than the recession itself is the vital fact that it has been superimposed upon an economy which, in the last few years, has been sluggish and tired.

Thus, anyone who thought in 1958 that all was well with the American economy just because the recession of that year bottomed out early was proved to be wrong by the sad fact that our last recovery was an anemic one: 1959 and 1960 have been grievously disappointing years, as the period of expansion proved both to be shorter than earlier postwar recoveries and to have been abortive in the sense of never carrying us back anywhere near to high employment and high capacity levels of operations.

This is illustrated by the striking fact that unemployment has remained above 5 per cent of the labor force, a most disappointing performance in comparison with earlier postwar recoveries and desirable social goals.

If what we now faced were only the case of a short recession that was imposed on an economy showing healthy growth and desirable high employment patterns, then governmental policies would have to be vastly different from those called for by the present outlook. But this is not 1949, nor 1954.

Prudent policy now requires that we also combat the basic sluggishness which underlies the more dramatic recession. In some ways a recession imposed on top of a disappointingly slack economy simplifies prudent decision-making.

Thus, certain expenditure programs that are worthwhile for their own sake, but that inevitably involve a lag of some months before they can get going, can be pushed more vigorously in the current situation because of the knowledge that the extra stimulus they later bring is unlikely to impinge upon a recovery that has already led us back to full employment.

The following recommendations try to take careful account of the fact that the recession slide is only the most dramatic manifestation of the grave economic challenge confronting our economic system.

II. FEASIBLE ECONOMIC GOALS

3. *Our Economic Potential.* Had our economy pro-
gressed since 1956—not at the dramatic sprint of the
Western European and Japanese economies or at the rush
of the controlled totalitarian systems, but simply at the
modest pace made possible by our labor force and productivity trends—we could have expected 1961 to bring
a Gross National Product some 10 per cent above the
$500,000,000,000 level we are now experiencing.

With unemployment below 4 per cent, with overcapacity
put to work, and with productivity unleashed by economic
opportunity, such a level of activity would mean higher
private consumption, higher corporate profits, higher capital formation for the future, and higher resources for
much-needed public programs.

Instead of our having now to debate about the size of
the budget deficit to be associated with a recession, such
an outcome would have produced tax revenues under our
present tax structure sufficient to lead to a surplus of
around $10,000,000,000; and the authorities might be fac-
ing the not unpleasant task of deciding how to deal with
such a surplus.

4. *The Targets Ahead.* Looking forward, one cannot
realistically expect to undo in 1961 the inadequacies of
several years. It is not realistic to aim for the restoration
of high employment within a single calendar year. The
goal for 1961 must be to bring the recession to an end, to
reinstate a condition of expansion and recovery and to
adopt measures likely to make that expansion one that
will not after a year or two peter out at levels of activity
far below our true potential.

Indeed, policy for 1961 should be directed against the
background of the whole decade ahead. Specifically, if the
American economy is to show healthy growth during this
period and to average out at satisfactory levels of employment, we must learn not to be misled by statements that
this or that is now at an all-time peak; in an economy like
ours, with more than 1,000,000 people coming into the labor force each year and with continuing technological
change, the most shocking frittering away of our economic opportunities is fully compatible with statistical re-

ports that employment and national product are "setting new records every year."

5. *Prudent Budget Goals.* A healthy decade of the Nineteen Sixties will not call for a budget that is exactly balanced in every fiscal year. For the period as a whole, if the forces making for expansion are strong and vigorous, there should be many years of budgetary surpluses and these may well have to exceed the deficits of other years. Economic forecasting of the far future is too difficult to make possible any positive statements concerning the desirable decade average of such surpluses and deficits. But careful students of sound economic fiscal policy will perhaps agree on the following:

(i) The first years of such a decade, characterized as they are by stubborn unemployment and excess capacity and following on a period of disappointing slackness, are the more appropriate periods for programs of economic stimulation by well-thought-out fiscal policy.

(ii) The unplanned deficits that result from recession-induced declines in tax receipts levied on corporate profits and individual incomes and also those that come from a carefully designed anti-recession program must be sharply distinguished from deficits that take place in times of zooming demand inflation. This last kind of deficit would represent Government spending out of control and be indeed deserving of grave concern. The deficits that come automatically from recession or which are a necessary part of a determined effort to restore the economic system to health are quite different phenomena: They are signs that our automatic built-in stabilizers are working, and that we no longer will run the risk of going into one of the great depressions that characterized our economic history before the war.

III. THE CONSTRAINTS WITHIN WHICH POLICY MUST WORK

6. *Gold and the International Payments.* Granted that the new Administration is preparing a whole series of measures to correct our balance of payments position, the days are gone when America could shape her domestic stabilization policies taking no thought for their international repercussions. The fact that we have been losing

gold for many years will, without question, have to affect our choice among activist policies to restore production and employment. The art of statecraft for the new Administration will be to innovate, within this recognized constraint, new programs that promote healthy recovery.

It would be unthinkable for a present-day American government to deliberately countenance high unemployment as a mechanism for adjusting to the balance of payments deficit.

Such a policy would be largely ineffective anyway; but even were it highly effective, only a cynic would counsel its acceptance. It is equally unthinkable that a responsible Administration can give up its militant efforts toward domestic recovery because of the limitations imposed on it by the international situation. What is needed is realistic taking into account of the international aspects of vigorous domestic policy.

7. The Problem of Inflation. Various experts, here and abroad, believe that the immediate postwar inflationary climate has now been converted into an epoch of price stability. One hopes this cheerful diagnosis is correct.

However, a careful survey of the behavior of prices and costs shows that our recent stability in the wholesale price index has come in a period of admittedly high unemployment and slackness in our economy. For this reason it is premature to believe that the restoration of high employment will no longer involve problems concerning the stability of prices.

Postwar experience, here and abroad, suggests that a mixed economy like ours may tend to generate an upward creep of prices before it arrives at high employment. Such a price creep, which has to be distinguished from the ancient inflations brought about by the upward pull on prices and wages that comes from excessive dollars of demand spending, has been given many names: "cost-push" inflation, "sellers" (rather than demanders) inflation, "market-power" inflation—these are all variants of the same stubborn phenomenon.

Economists are not yet agreed how serious this new malady of inflation really is. Many feel that new institutional programs, other than conventional fiscal and monetary policies, must be devised to meet this new challenge.

But whatever be the merits of the varying views on this subject, it should be manifest that the goal of high employment and effective real growth cannot be abandoned because of the problematical fear that re-attaining of prosperity in America may bring with it some difficulties; if recovery means a reopening of the cost-push problem, then we have no choice but to move closer to the day when that problem has to be successfully grappled with. Economic statesmanship does involve difficult compromises, but not capitulation to any one of the pluralistic goals of modern society.

Running a deliberately slack economy in order to put off the day when such doubts about inflation can be tested is not a policy open to a responsible democratic government in this decade of perilous world crisis. A policy of inaction can be as truly a policy of living dangerously as one of overaction. Far from averting deterioration of our international position, a program that tolerates stagnation in the American economy can prevent us from making those improvements in our industrial productivity that are so desperately needed if we are to remain competitive in the international markets of the world.

History reminds us that even in the worst days of the Great Depression there was never a shortage of experts to warn against all curative public actions, on the ground that they were likely to create a problem of inflation. Had this counsel prevailed here, as it did in pre-Hitler Germany, the very existence of our form of government could be at stake. No modern government will make that mistake again.

IV. GENERAL POLICY RECOMMENDATIONS

8. *Introduction.* The two principal governmental weapons to combat recession and slackness are fiscal (i.e., tax and expenditure) policy and monetary or credit policy. In ordinary times both should be pushed hard, so that they are reinforcing rather than conflicting. These are not ordinary times. Until our new programs have taken effect, America does not have the freedom from balance of payments constraints that she enjoyed for the twenty-five years after 1933.

The usual balance between fiscal and monetary policies

will have to be shifted in the period just ahead toward a more vigorous use of fiscal policy because of the international constraint.

Some of the conventional mechanisms of credit policy may have to be altered to meet the new situation we face. While credit was made very easy in the 1954 and 1958 recessions in order to induce housing and other investment spending, a similar reduction of the short-term interest rate on Government bills down to the 1 per cent level might lead in 1961 to a further movement of international funds to foreign money markets, thereby intensifying our gold drains. Because our monetary institutions are slowly evolving ones, the following recommendations deal less fully with monetary policy than the subject deserves in a full-scale study of stabilization.

9. *The Need for Flexibility.* Since experience shows that no one can forecast the economic future with pinpoint accuracy, the policy maker cannot plan for a single course of action; he must be prepared with a list of programs, reserving some on the list for the contingency that events in the early months of 1961 may turn out somewhat worse than what today seems to be the most likely outcome. The following recommendations of this report, therefore, fall into two parts.

First come those minimal measures that need to be pushed hard even if the current recession turns out to be one that can be reversed by next summer at the latest. Expansions and accelerations in expenditure programs that are desirable for their own sake, improvements in unemployment compensation, new devices that permit use of flexible credit policy within the international constraints, and stimulus to residential housing are examples of measures that belong in our first line of defense and which are already seen to be justified by what we know about the recent behavior of the American economy. Now in January the wisdom of such policies can already be verified.

Second comes a list of other measures of expansion which represent sound programs to combat a sagging economy, but which are more controversial at this time. If we could read the future better, they might be just what is now needed.

But given our limitations, it may be safer to hold such

measures in reserve. As the months pass, and the February and March facts become available, we shall be in a position to know whether more vigorous actions are called for. Flexibility in decision-making deserves emphasis: There is nothing inconsistent about asking for measures in March that one does not ask for in January, if events have provided us with new information in the meantime. The annual budget should itself be a "living document." Just as Congress should begin to explore measures that will enhance the flexibility of tax rates by giving certain discretionary powers to the Executive, so should Congress itself be quite prepared to flexibly reverse its field in tax legislation when new economic conditions are recognized to call for new measures.

10. *Important Warnings.* It is just as important to know what not to do as to know what to do. What definitely is not called for in the present situation is a massive program of hastily devised public works whose primary purpose is merely that of making jobs and getting money pumped into the economy. The Roosevelt New Deal inherited a bankrupt economy that was in desperate straits. Whatever the wisdom of anti-depression "make work" projects in such an environment, they are definitely not called for at the present time. There is so much that America needs in the way of worthwhile governmental programs and modern stabilization has so many alternative weapons to fight depression as to make it quite unnecessary to push the panic button and resort to inefficient spending devices.

Similarly, as was mentioned earlier, massive spending programs designed to undo in a year the inadequacies of several years do not represent desirable fiscal policy. Planned deficits, like penicillin and other antibiotics, have their appropriate place in our cabinet of economic health measures; but just as the doctor carries things too far when he prescribes antibiotics freely and without thought of proper dosage, so too does the modern government err in the direction of activism when it goes all out and calls for every conceivable kind of anti-recession policy. The golden mean between inaction and overaction is hard to define, and yet it must be resolutely sought.

Finally, it is worth repeating the warning against concentrating exclusively on ending a downward slide of activity and ignoring the suboptimal level at which the economy may then be operating. Even if this recession ended early in 1961, and even if its initial stages seemed to show a tolerable rate of improvement, that would not alone be enough to render unnecessary policies aimed to get us back to, and keep us at, high employment levels.

Satisfactory growth is not something one procures by a once-and-for-all act; eternal vigilance, as with so many other good things, is the price that must be paid for good economic performance.

V. "FIRST LINE OF DEFENSE" POLICIES

11. *Expenditure Programs.* Pledged expenditure programs that are desired for their own sake should be pushed hard. If 1961-62 had threatened to be years of over-full-employment and excessive inflationary demand, caution might require going a little easy on some of them. The opposite is in prospect. The following measures are not being advocated in the faith that they will help business from declining in the first months of the new year. Some of them will, at best, pay out money only after a considerable delay. They are advocated for their own sakes as builders of a better, fairer, and faster-growing economy.

And even should their expenditures come into play after we have reversed the recession tide, they should be helpful in making the next recovery a truly satisfactory and lasting one.

(i) Defense expenditures ought to be determined on their own merits. They are not to be the football of economic stabilization. Nor, as was so often done in the past, ought they to be kept below the optimal level needed for security because of the mistaken notion that the economy is unable to bear any extra burdens.

Certainly a recession drop in tax receipts should not inhibit vital expenditures any more than should the operation of artificial limits on the public debt. And they should certainly not be maintained at high levels merely for the purpose of substitution for other measures designed to keep employment high.

On the other hand, any stepping up of these programs

that is deemed desirable for its own sake can only help rather than hinder the health of our economy in the period immediately ahead.

(ii) Foreign aid is likewise to be determined by the need for development abroad. An increase in this program, skillfully tailored to take account of the international payment position, deserves high national priority in a period like this one.

(iii) Education programs including funds for school construction, teachers' salaries, increased loans for college dormitories should be vigorously pushed. Some of these could have an impact even within calendar year 1961 itself.

(iv) Urban renewal programs, including slum clearance and improvement of transportation facilities, represent desirable projects that should come high on the policy agenda.

(v) Health and welfare programs, including medical care of the aged, increased grants for hospital construction, and continued large grants for medical research, are desirable even though some of them—such as health for the aged financed by social security—will not add at all to dollar demand in the near future.

(vi) Improved unemployment compensation is one of the most important of all the measures on this list from the standpoint of anti-recession action.

The fairest and most effective step the Federal Government can take to help fight the recession would be to expand unemployment compensation benefits. Such expenditures go to those who need them and who will spend the money promptly; they also go up at the right time and in the right place and will come down at the right time and in the right place. It is a sad fact, however, that the nation's unemployment compensation system cannot possibly do the job it is expected to do. Under present arrangements, it was shown to be inadequate in the 1957-58 recession and it will be inadequate in the present recession as well.

For the immediate future, emergency legislation is needed to permit all states to continue paying unemployment benefits (perhaps at a stepped-up rate) for at least thirty-nine weeks, regardless of the condition of their insurance reserves and even if they have not yet repaid the loans received to tide them over in 1958.

For the long pull, we need a system with basic Federal standards that will cover employees in all firms regardless of size; provide unemployment benefits of at least one half of the employee's earnings; and extend the term of benefits to a minimum of twenty-six weeks in all states, supplemented by an additional thirteen weeks during periods of high national unemployment. Federal standards are also needed to provide for adequate financing and solvency of the system.

Consideration should also be given to the possibility of equalizing the burden of financing unemployment benefits among the states, and to varying the benefits in such a way that they will go up when unemployment in the nation as a whole is high and go down when unemployment is low. These measures would reinforce the stabilizing effectiveness of the system in all stages of the business cycle and would eliminate the need for hasty action during periods of emergency.

(vii) Useful public works programs should be accelerated. Cement capacity and labor availability are such as to execution. This applies to Federal and Federally supported programs, such as water resources, highways, post office construction, public building construction by the General Services Administration and military construction.

Prompt additional appropriations and authorizations by the Congress are needed in most cases. Opportunities for speeding up authorized public works exist also at the state and local levels. Cooperation of all levels of Government strengthens an anti-recession program.

(viii) Highway construction programs can be accelerated. Cement capacity and labor availability are such as to make this a potent near-term stimulant.

An aggressive Federal highway program might involve any of the following measures: Relaxing contract controls over state obligations, and assuring states their obligations will be met; authorizing repayable advance to the states to meet their 10 per cent matching requirements under the Interstate program; waiving the pay-as-you-go amendment if required to permit full apportionment of future

Interstate authorizations and, if deemed necessary, increase these authorizations.

(ix) Depressed area programs are desirable both in the short run and the long. The Douglas Report spells out needs in this matter and makes comment unnecessary here.

(x) Natural resource development projects, including conservation and recreation facilities, provide further examples of useful programs.

The above list does not pretend to be exhaustive. Certain other expenditures measures could be added to a first line of defense program, but enough has been said to indicate the nature of the needed actions. The order of magnitude contemplated here might be in the neighborhood of $3,000,000,000 to $5,000,000,000 above already planned programs in fiscal 1962 and does not involve the inflationary risks of an all-out anti-recession blitzkrieg. This does not purport to make up for the accumulative deficiencies in those vital areas.

12. *Residential Housing Stimulus.* The last two recessions were helped immensely by a successful program to make credit more available to residential housing. No experts could have predicted the anti-cyclical potency that housing has shown in the post-war period.

Already we have seen some easing of credit in this area, but such steps do not seem this time to have been so successful in coaxing out a new demand for home construction. There is perhaps some reason to fear that less can be expected from the housing area in the year ahead. Down payments are already quite low, as are monthly payments. Vacancy rates, particularly in certain areas and for certain types of housing, have been rising. The age brackets that provide the greatest demand for new housing are hollow ones because of the dearth of births during the depression of the Nineteen Thirties.

Nonetheless, so great is the need for housing a few years from now when the wartime babies move into the house-buying brackets and so useful is the stimulation that a resurgence of housing could bring that it would seem folly not to make a determined effort in this area. In particular, loans for modernization of homes, which now bear so high an interest rate, might provide a promising source for expansion.

Many specific actions will be required. Mortgage rates might be brought down to, say, 4½ per cent interest, with discounts on mortgages correspondingly reduced; consideration might be given to further extended maximum amortization periods. The insurance fee for single dwellings under Federal Housing Administration programs might well be reduced from ½ per cent to ¼ per cent.

The Federal National Mortgage Association (F.N.M.A. or "Fannie May") could step up its mortgage purchasing program, especially for high-risk mortgages lacking private markets. Housing for the elderly is another program desirable for its own sake. Measures that tie in with urban renewal and college dormitories, as covered above, also hold out promise.

Particularly because our international balance of payments inhibits certain types of activistic monetary policy will it be necessary to push hard on specific credit programs in the housing field. Innovation, ingenuity and experimentation with new instrumentalities will be needed in this matter: It is not reasonable to believe that the patterns earlier arrived at are the last word in feasible programming.

13. *The Role of Monetary Policy.* Were it not for the international constraint, an economy that faced recession in the short run and which had been falling below its potential for several years would naturally call for a considerable easing of credit. Indeed, a growth-oriented program would entail a combination of low interest rates and widely available credit with an austere fiscal program designed to create budget surpluses large enough to offset any resulting overstimulation of demand. But such a program must await a solution of our international economic difficulties that will free our hands in domestic monetary policy.

The first order of business is to get nearer to high employment. Expansion by the Federal Reserve of bank reserves, in order to increase the supply of money and to stimulate investment spending, will naturally tend to lower short-term interest rates. But in view of the volatility of funds as between our money markets and those abroad which pay higher interest, we can plan only limited use of this conventional mechanism. New exploration is needed.

(i) In the days after the 1951 Accord, when the lesson had to be learned that Government bonds were not in peacetime to be arbitrarily pegged at artificial price levels, it was perhaps defensible for the monetary authorities to concentrate almost wholly on open market operations in the shortest-term Government securities.

Without entering into the merits of this position—and the problem is indeed anything but a simple one to be decided by emotional slogans—responsible economists realize that the new international situation requires some change in emphasis. Indeed, it is encouraging to note that the Federal Reserve authorities have themselves already been experimenting with actions designed to adjust to the new situation.

Still further actions may be desirable in order to help bring long-term interest rates down relative to short-term. It is long-term rates which are most decisive for investment spending; and it is short-term interest rates that are most decisive for foreign balances. This is not an area for hasty improvisation or doctrinaire reversal of policies; but it is one for pragmatic evolutions of procedures and policies.

Nor is this merely a task for the Federal Reserve. The Treasury too must consider the wisdom of relying primarily on short-term issues in the period just ahead. Those in Congress who have thought that recession times are the best period in which to issue long-term debt at low interest rates will have to go through the same agonizing reappraisal of their view as a result of the new international situation.

The whole problem of debt management by the Treasury, as coordinated with the Federal Reserve in the interest of over-all stability, will require rethinking in these new times. No conflict of desires between the Executive and the Federal Reserve is to be involved, since both have the same interest in economic recovery and defense of the dollar.

(ii) Decisive actions to improve our international balance of payments position are desired for their own sake as well as to liberate domestic stabilization policies. This is not the place to describe the numerous programs that are needed in the international area.

Fortunately, there are some reasons to think that our net export position is an improving one and that the task is not an impossibly difficult one. The primary need is to make sure that our productivity is improved so that our costs will remain competitive in international markets. But there are also certain measures that can alleviate the psychological drain on gold.

VI. "SECOND LINE OF DEFENSE" POLICIES

14. *Two Alternatives.* All the above has been premised upon a specific, and perhaps optimistic, forecast of how the economy is likely to behave in 1961. This first alternative could be called the "optimistic model" were it not for the fact that it turns out to involve unemployment that does not shrink much or any in 1961 below present levels of some 6 per cent. It seems, nevertheless, to agree most closely with the likeliest expectations revealed by a careful canvass of economic forecasters in business firms, universities, and public agencies.

Concretely, the optimistic model assumes that the Gross National Product will decline for at most one or two quarters. It assumes that the calendar year G. N. P. will average out to between $510,000,000,000 and $515,000,000,000, which represents an improvement in real G. N. P. of about 2 per cent in money terms and 1 per cent in real terms (after correction for price changes has been made).

It assumes that by the end of the year the economy will be running some 3 per cent above the present rate. It assumes that even in the absence of any needed programs by the new Administration the current budget will have lost its surplus and more likely will show some deficit. It assumes that our new jobs will be barely enough to provide work for the 1,200,000 workers who are added to the labor force in 1961 and that unemployment remains a grave social problem.

Evidently such an outlook cannot be regarded as an optimistic one; and it is to improve upon this situation that the above programs were prescribed.

It is only wise, though, to be prepared for an even worse outlook. Suppose inventory decumulation continues longer than expected above; that consumers continue to save as large a percentage of their disposable incomes as they have recently been doing; that plant and equipment expenditures by business accelerate their downward slide; and that construction generally proves to be disappointing. What then?

In that case unemployment will rise toward and perhaps beyond the critical $7\frac{1}{2}$ per cent level that marks that peak of the post-war era. In that case corporate profits will sink far below their present depressed levels, and a sagging stock market may add to the public's feeling of pessimism.

In that case we shall certainly automatically incur a large deficit. While many hope and expect this more pessimistic model will not happen, it cannot be ruled out by careful students of economic history and present indications.

15. *A Temporary Tax Cut.* If economic reports on business during the early months of the year begin to suggest that the second, more pessimistic outlook, is the more relevant one, then it will be the duty of public policy to take a more active, expansionary role. This is not the place to spell out the details of such a program. But certainly the following tax-cut measure will then deserve consideration.

A temporary reduction in tax rates on individual incomes can be a powerful weapon against recession. Congress could legislate, for example, a cut of 3 or 4 percentage points in the tax rate applicable to every income class, to take effect immediately under our withholding system in March or April and to continue until the end of the year.

In view of the great desirability of introducing greater flexibility into tax rates, it would be highly desirable for Congress to grant to the Executive the right to continue such a reduction for one or two six-month (or three-month) periods beyond that time (subject to the actions being set aside by joint resolution of Congress) with the clear understanding that the reduction will definitely expire by the end of 1962.

At this time it would be urgently important to make sure that any tax cut was clearly a temporary one. With the continued international uncertainty and with new public programs coming up in the years ahead, sound finance may require a maintenance of our present tax structure and any weakening of it in order to fight a recession might be tragic.

Even if it should prove to be the case that growth makes reduction of tax rates possible in the long run, that should be a decision taken on its own merits and adopted along with a comprehensive reforming of our present tax structure. (Various tax devices to stimulate investment might also be part of a comprehensive program designed to eliminate loopholes, promote equity, and enhance incentives.)

16. *Direct Attack on the Wage-Price Spiral.* The above programs have been primarily concerned with fiscal and monetary policy. This is as it should be.

It is important, though, to realize that there are some problems that fiscal and monetary policy cannot themselves come to grips with. Thus, if there is indeed a tendency for prices and wages to rise long before we reach high employment, neither monetary nor fiscal policy can be used to the degree necessary to promote desired growth.

What may then be needed are new approaches to the problem of productivity, wages, and price formation. Will it not be possible to bring government influence to bear on this vital matter without invoking direct controls on wages and prices?

Neither labor, nor management, nor the consumer can gain from an increase in price tags. Just as we pioneered in the Nineteen Twenties in creating potent monetary mechanisms and in the Nineteen Thirties in forging the tools of effective fiscal policy, so may it be necessary in the Nineteen Sixties to meet head on the problem of a price creep.

This is a challenge to mixed economies all over the free world, and is not to be met by government alone.